Praise for The Empath Leader

"*The Empath Leader* is a transformative and essential read for anyone aspiring to make a meaningful impact in today's world. This book is more than a guide; it's a mirror reflecting our immense potential to lead with compassion, intuition, and emotional intelligence.

The personal stories, combined with the insightful Cs of Empath Leadership, deeply resonated with me, invigorating my commitment to this empathic leadership revolution. This compelling work is a critical tool for anyone ready to harness their empathic abilities to inspire, influence, and create a more connected world."

- Alex Raymond, Host of The Conscious Entrepreneur Summit and The Conscious Entrepreneur Podcast

"Where many leadership books teach you to lead within existing frameworks, *The Empath Leader* is here to disrupt the status quo. It calls for a revolution, where leadership truly lies in the hands of the people and the ability to thrive isn't reserved for the elite — it's democratized. *The Empath Leader* doesn't just make you think, it compels you into empowered, human-centered action that stems from within."

- Annie Petsche, Coach for Multi-Passionate Change-Makers & Future of Work Thought Leader

"*The Empath Leader* takes the broad notion of what it means to be an empath *and* a leader and examines, defines, and substantiates its constituent parts. It handles ideas methodically, introducing taxonomies, situating histories, and citing contemporary business sources to connect with and uplevel the awareness of its readers.

The Empath Leader does all that without being inaccessible or sterile. The work is enriched by stories, quotes, and reflections that draw broadly from influences like French impressionism, Sufi mysticism, and the better angels of the 21st century self-help genre. If you are curious about how the approach of an Empath Leader might deepen your impact and change your world, or just wanting for new vocabulary to understand yourself, read this book."

- Tony Morales, Co-Founder and Chairman of Prepory College Admissions Counseling

The Empath Leader
Your Ultimate Guide to Authentic Influence

Claudia Cauterucci

with **Kayleigh O'Keefe**

with **Carmen Berkley**

with **Charles Martinez**

with **Felicia Ortiz**

Edited by **Kecia Bal**

The Empath Leader: Your Ultimate Guide to Authentic Influence

Copyright © 2024 by Claudia Cauterucci & Soul Excellence Publishing

Print ISBN: 979-8-9883816-7-9

Digital ISBN: 979-8-9883816-6-2

All rights reserved.

No part of this book may be reproduced in any form or by any electronic or mechanical means, including information storage and retrieval systems, without written permission from the author, except for the use of brief quotations in a book review.

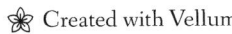 Created with Vellum

Contents

The Empath Leader Origin Story 1

Part One
The Empath Leader

1. When Worlds Collide 9
2. Meet The Empath 16
3. Three Types of Empaths 29
4. Rooted in Power 39
5. Self-Care: Your Survival Kit 48
6. What Kind of Psychic Are You? 63
7. Build Your Bridge to Leadership 81
8. Narcissists on the Prowl 92
9. A Paradigm Shift 107
10. The Heart of Leadership 122
11. Leadership and The Rise of The Meek 129
12. My Own Empath Leader Story 140
    Meet Claudia Cauterucci 153

Part Two
Stories From Empath Leaders

13. YOUR SACRED REBELLION 157
    Kayleigh O'Keefe

    Meet Kayleigh O'Keefe 173

14. THE CARE BEAR MODEL OF LEADERSHIP 175
    Carmen Berkley

    Meet Carmen Berkley 197

15. HUMAN PIÑATA 199
    Charles Martinez

Meet Charles Martinez	213
16. LEADING EDUCATION WITH LOVE Felicia Ortiz	215
Meet Felicia Ortiz	227

Part Three
The Ultimate Empath Leadership Toolkit

Modalities for Enhancing Your Intuition and Connection to the Divine	231
Claudisms	239
Acknowledgments	245
Bibliography	249
Also By Soul Excellence Publishing	253

The Empath Leader Origin Story
A Letter From the Publisher

A Meeting of Hearts and Minds

Have you ever met someone, but not really *seen* them until much later? That's how I feel about Claudia Cauterucci, the lead author of *The Empath Leader*.

In 2021, I decided to make a huge investment. I signed up for a year-long mastermind to learn how to build a speaking-based business. For the 18 months prior, I had been building Soul Excellence Publishing and on a mission to amplify the wisdom of conscious leadership. I knew the next phase for me was to share my own message, to present, to inspire, to speak, to use my voice. Little did I know that someone else had a similar dream. Her name was Claudia Cauterucci.

After 20 years of practicing as a psychotherapist and developing her own modalities for healing, she too, was ready to leap onto the big stage. Our big hearts and our shared ambition brought us together, and we spent the year meeting biweekly online and quarterly in person for four days of intensive communing and co-creating.

We slowly got to know one another. At our first meeting, Claudia revealed her profound psychic gifts as she helped another participant navigate a particularly difficult moment. Claudia later saw my promise as we spent the weekend in Flagstaff, Arizona, where I devised an idea for a women's leadership retreat and shared my big energy in a silent dance party and hike through the Grand Canyon.

But it wasn't until an overseas trip to Italy that we *saw* each other for the first time. During a break in the action, we wandered through the ancient town of Montelparo, resting high on a hill on Italy's Adriatic coast. We entered an old church and descended into the crypt, finding ourselves in front of a beautiful statue of Mary. In that moment, we felt a deep connection, a long-lost sisterhood.

And we both realized that there was a grand design behind our meeting. Tears formed in our eyes as we were taken by the beauty, the history, and the significance of the unveiling–of seeing each other in this new way. As we ended the year, we understood that our journey had not been about starting a speaking-based business but rather meeting each other and experiencing the empath-narcissist dynamic, a theme central to this book, and realizing that it was time for the Empath to rise.

The Birth of The Empath Leader

I like to think of the first year of our friendship as the cosmic egg that brought us together. The second year could be described as a mutual sharing of the gifts we had perceived

The Empath Leader Origin Story

in one another. For example, I was putting out a book called *The Diversity in Humanity,* and Claudia joined the project, contributing a remarkable chapter on healing and connection called "Humanity 101: A Colorful Journey Home to Care." I then experienced Claudia's full gifts by joining her inaugural Empath Leader Training. My life would never be the same. Suddenly, everything made sense. My intuition, my sensitivity, my big heart—these were not liabilities. They were my biggest assets, but I had ignored them. I hungrily ate up Claudia's insights and practical tools for leading as an empath and knew something was still gestating in the cosmic egg of our co-creation.

As our friendship entered our third year, we wondered aloud on hours-long Zoom calls about how to move toward the New Earth without getting lost in dismantling the old. With *cafecitos* in hand, we brainstormed idea after idea Sunday after Sunday on how to collaborate together until one appeared: *The Empath Leader* book.

It was almost too obvious!

What better way to refine the teachings, spark an awakening of Empaths worldwide, and tap into our unique Zones of Genius to create together? We were dead-set on not doing this alone as publisher and lead author. We knew we had to call in powerhouse reinforcements, fellow Empath Leaders who not only had completed Claudia's training but were ready and willing to be more visible and vocal about their empathic gifts and their visions for the future. Authors **Carmen Berkley**, **Charles Martinez**, and **Felicia Ortiz** answered the call.

For months, we have gathered together to write, share, and collaborate on the book you now hold in your hands. The

Claudia Cauterucci

fire heart emoji symbol featured on the cover emerged one night on a group call as the primary symbol of the Empath - passionate, heartfelt, and visible. The idea for Claudia to host each of us on her multi-dimensional *Heaven on Earth* podcast emerged on another call. We had created the space–the book–and magic flowed through it.

With Claudia at the helm sharing her teachings, each of us has joined in to express how our personal journey as an Empath Leader has unfolded. It is my sincere hope that you walk away from this book with three things:

1. A deep understanding of what it means to be both an Empath and Empath Leader;
2. A set of tools and practices you can use to start embracing your innate gifts as an Empath Leader;
3. A sense of connection as you see yourself in the stories of awakening and leadership we share.

Our journey is no longer just our own. It's a shared path, a party of "two-niverse," one of the many *Claudisms* that are pure Empath - clever, cute, and concise. It's us and the universe in constant communion and co-creation. (You can find a whole section of Claudia's Claudisms in the back of this book.)

I have been building a bridge - book by book - from the old way to the new. Over the last four years, I have published 17 bestselling books on leadership featuring over 500 unique authors from 16 countries through my company, Soul Excellence Publishing. This book, *The Empath Leader*, represents the culmination of that deep exploration and connection with so many people. *The Empath Leader*, I believe, is the overarching umbrella that best describes *who*

The Empath Leader Origin Story

Soul Excellence has published - Empath Leaders - and *what our mission has been all along* - Heaven on Earth.

I am forever grateful to Claudia for sharing her wisdom with me and choosing me to bring her wisdom to life in *The Empath Leader,* which will have an everlasting impact. More than that, I am grateful for her witness; she notices and speaks to the things that make me special. And I am grateful for her endless well of patience and encouragement as I often came close to throwing in the towel on this mission over the years. Thank you.

At the end of each Empath Leader training session over the course of 12 weeks, Claudia invited us to close with each person going around the Zoom room, making eye contact, and saying goodnight. I'll modify it slightly here to express my gratitude for my collaborators and you, dear reader, for being here with us:

> Thank you, Felicia.
> Thank you, Charles.
> Thank you, Carmen.
> Thank you, Claudia.

And thank you, reader. Thank YOU, Empath Leader.

With love and gratitude and a fiery heart,

Kayleigh O'Keefe

Founder and CEO of Soul Excellence Publishing

Part One
The Empath Leader

Chapter 1
When Worlds Collide

*"Art is not what you see,
but what you make others see."*

— Edgar Degas

The Great Shift

We find ourselves in a great overlap between two worlds and in the midst of a demarcation of two eras: life before 2020 and life after 2020.

The world, post-pandemic, finds itself in the throes of monumental questioning of tradition, policy, hierarchy, power, systems, and beliefs. Individuals all over the world are demanding the right to authenticity, protagonism, self-governance, and unparalleled freedom of expression, magnified through access to internet connectivity and translated into extraordinary *human* connectivity.

Claudia Cauterucci

We are all responsive witnesses to slight and gargantuan shifts all over the planet as if swaying back and forth to a call-and-response chant.

Centuries of belief are collapsing. The givens of the pre-pandemic world, rooted in protocols that have always been questioned and resisted, today are being pulled down from the center square. What was dissatisfaction pre-pandemic has morphed into an all-out rage, and these practices will just no longer do:

- the pursuit of power for its own sake;
- power grounded in irrational constructs like skin color and economic supremacy;
- top-heavy financial hierarchy, with pages of fine-print irrespective of merit;
- a blind adherence to tradition, where obligation trumps effectiveness;
- a stark and painful divorce between science and spirituality, with science (the material) superseding all things spiritual (the energetic);
- an unabashed domination and exploitation of nature, encompassing all coexisting beings, humans, and animals alike;
- the glorification of exaggerated male traits, disrupting balance and equanimity for BOTH men and women, as they are asked to abandon connective parts of themselves; and
- decisions driven by the intellect, relegating heart-based intuition to the realm of "soft skills" and "woo."

These revolutions have always happened, you might say. Yes, in France all by itself, in Russia over there, in the U.S. back then. But today, we have the internet, a GoPro camera on the forehead of humanity that allows us to see everything that's going on around us. The internet, our human neural network, has brought our pains and joys, our dark and our light, into every single home, every corner, every village, every bar stool. We can not look away.

Trauma Explosions

The pandemic not only created layers of fresh trauma but also triggered a planetary explosion of buried trauma, exposed fault lines, and erupted deep, dark gunk that now floods the Netflix documentaries category. As in all moments of "going inside"—which the pandemic forced us to do—a veil of unconsciousness lifted, and the acknowledgment and validation of historical human trauma unleashed a torrent of open air discussions where nothing is taboo.

As pendulum swings go, however, it has also created undulation after undulation of healing discussions, forums, circles, round tables, red tables, podcasts, and books such as this one. Healing is the name of the game, and as far as I am concerned, we are the better for it. This new era befits the old adage, "The wise man is the rooster of the universe: he awakens the unawake."

This Phoenix moment embodies both demise and resurgence, the natural cycle of death and rebirth, and if we look hard enough, we can find the everlasting essence of the soul. If we can withstand the pains and messiness of childbirth and engage our breathing, a beautiful rebirth is at hand.

Claudia Cauterucci

Centuries of humanity's routines for dealing with themselves, others, and the planet are in upheaval, and if this time were a tarot card, it definitely is the Tower, which in its crumbling, also promises a beginning.

We are at the "go" square on this life board game, and the *a priori* question is, "How should humans be human now?"

A Time to Lead the R-Evolution

This overlap has a *Lord of the Flies* agitation, an island ambushed by teenagers running amuck, trying to self-govern in a land unbeknownst to them. The pressure to evolve at this high speed is overwhelming. The pairing of unprecedented evolution juxtaposed with a faint smell of war lurking right around the next corner is disconcerting at best and terrifying at worst. Remaining unconscious is not an option.

Avoiding self-reflection promises a war that will lead us to extinction. On the other hand, hitting bottom has no place to go but up, and "up," in humanity's case, means an opportunity for evolution. I like to call this a "Dynamic R-Evolution." Dynamic because this moment is buzzing with energy, activity, and, crossing fingers, progress. R-Evolution, because we are in the midst of a dramatic change (a revolution) with some overthrows, yes, but with one hand reaching for the summit of evolution.

If we uncomfortably flex into these winds of change, this Dynamic R-Evolution will uplevel us all, starting with the individual. Your healing is the healing of the planet. Your rising from the ashes is OUR renaissance.

This correlation is true for any individual, but the impact grows exponentially for Empaths who choose healing.

In these chaotic times, people are looking for leaders, guides, coaches, therapists, and advisors who can help them find meaning and purpose in this new planetary landscape. From an attachment theory perspective, planet Earth and its human children need some secure parenting right ... about ... now.

This post-pandemic era is asking for leaders who know themselves emotionally, who value high empathy, and who are able to foment a healthy emotional daily life environment. Today, we have an urgent need for leaders who show up authentically, are unafraid of their vulnerabilities yet shine in their strengths, validate internal experiences, and inspire others. Humans, the planet, and the times are crying out for a new type of leader who can respond to a turbulent environment using intuition, self-reflection, compassion, and emotional intelligence.

In my view, this is the exact description of good parenting: kind yet firm, internally and externally attuned, solid and sensitive, serious and fun. We need these characteristics to help us feel securely attached to our future.

I propose that the Empath Leader engenders all of these outcomes.

An Invitation to Heal

In this book, we are going to explore the Empath Leader on many levels and layers—all part of a multidisciplinary approach that I've seen work true miracles.

Claudia Cauterucci

As a multidimensional therapist, coach, and guide, I connect to the people I work with in multi-phasic ways: I connect on an earthly level or three-dimensionally; I connect clinically, within diagnostic parameters; I connect tactically, using tools, psychological theory, and somatic practices; and I connect holistically, with the heart and the Spirit, in whatever form that appears. My multiculturalism also allows me to have a broader view of cultural beliefs, ancient traditions, and practices.

It's my honor to guide you—whether you see yourself as an Empath or whether you are a curious, open-hearted human —through the complexities of healing ourselves and therefore sparking healing on a much broader level. If you feel called to leadership, I will guide you there. Or you may simply be interested in understanding the leadership qualities that will help create a better world. Through this book, I will be talking both *about* Empaths and Empath Leaders and, at times, *directly to* Empaths and Empath Leaders—but I'm also talking to anyone who has an interest in the changes unfolding around us. If you care enough about humanity to pick up this book, I'm talking to you.

To Empaths, my promise is bold, but I know it will ring true if you allow the message to come through. I'm here to tell you that we Empaths are born hardwired with the ability to not only absorb unseen energies but also to distinguish them, tame them, and train them into our superpower.

Here's a quick look at where we're going together. If this book was a Venn diagram, the first chapters in the left circle move internally to cover all things Empath. As we explore the nature and the needs of the Empath, I'll be giving you the tools—the "bricks," if you will—to build the bridge to

When Worlds Collide

Empath Leadership. The right circle moves us back out into the world with a leadership perspective, complete with an array of insight from Empath Leaders and lightworkers with whom I am delighted to share these pages.

And, in the middle—the element that brings both pieces together—the big, vibrant, and fierce *kind heart* is the connector that brings it all together. Let's begin our journey.

Chapter 2
Meet The Empath

"Knowledge is power; power provides information; information leads to education, education breeds wisdom; wisdom is liberation."

— Israelmore Ayivor

If these global changes feel overwhelming to you on a deeply personal level, this book is the start of your wisdom journey as an Empath.

As Socrates said, "To know thyself is the beginning of wisdom." Knowing shapes us on an individual and a collective level across history. Poverty stems from a profound sense of not knowing. The Dark Ages are marked by the gap between those who knew and those who didn't know. Knowing ourselves gives us power and ultimately, liberation.

If your intuition is telling you that you may be an Empath—well, welcome to the Ph.D. on you.

The Difference Between Empathy and Being an Empath

This is a good place to mark the difference between having empathy and being an Empath.

I capitalize the "e" in Empath because I use it as a proper noun. Empaths are not just humans with high empathy. I speak of them as a subsection of human society that feels to me like a lost tribe with their own characteristics, psychological etiology, pourquoi story, common language, and value system when interacting with other humans, animals, and their biosphere.

Empathy and being an Empath are related concepts, but they have distinct meanings. Empathy refers to the ability to understand and share the feelings of another person. It involves being able to put oneself in someone else's shoes, perceive their emotions, and respond in a way that acknowledges and validates those feelings. Empathy is a fundamental aspect of our human connective tissue, and it is crucial for building connections and relationships. There are different types of empathy, including:

1. Cognitive empathy: understanding another person's perspective,
2. Emotional empathy: feeling what another person feels, and
3. Compassionate empathy: being moved to help others in distress.

The Empath has all three—and then some.

Claudia Cauterucci

Empathy is part of our human operating system—our human technology—— in that it forms an invisible connective thread that serves to bring us together in our sameness. Mirror neurons—the group of neurons that specialize in language, empathy, and social imitation—are the invisible mechanical push buttons that allow us to feel the emotions of others and exist exclusively to advance interrelatedness. When someone loses a loved one or a fur creature, our mirror neurons hone in on their grief and send an internal signal where we then reassure them as an empathic and relational response. We offer our support via hugs, presence, meatloafs, and phone calls. The beauty of empathy is that we don't have to know the other human; we just acknowledge that they *are* human and that shared emotions are what make us human.

Sameness through shared emotion has helped us survive as a species. Empathy initiates care. Without empathy in the form of emergency shelters, hospitals, child care, first responders, roadside assistance from strangers, and sandwiches for the homeless at the 7-Eleven, we humans would have gone extinct a long time ago. Empathy fills our heart and *is* our heart. Empathy is at the core of what it means to be human. It is indisputable: empathy in the form of care is central to our existence. Full stop.

✳ ✳ ✳

Personal share: I have the most beautiful memory of empathy. I was driving home with my 4-year-old and I noticed that the gas light was blinking pretty hard. I picked up my speed to get to the gas station that was two blocks from my house. My car began put-puttering, and I fixated

Meet The Empath

on not looking anxious so that my child wouldn't get alarmed. Lo and behold, my car stopped 1,000 feet or so from the gas station. Next to me was a pick-up truck with four Latino construction workers. They saw that I was stopped in the middle of the road. Without hesitation, without my asking, they jumped out of their truck, gave each other instructions in Spanish—they clearly had constructed a game plan—and started pushing my car toward the gas station. Once I was safe and well positioned to fill the tank, and following my profuse thanks, they refused the little cash I offered, ran back to their pick-up, and zoomed off. I'm in tears just remembering it. Empathy.

An Empath, on the other hand, is a person who is particularly sensitive to the emotions and energy of others. They feel the room, not just the person standing next to them. They possess a heightened and deepened capacity for empathy that does not even require seeing a person, just sensing them. Empaths absorb the emotions of those around them to an unusual degree. Being an Empath is a more intense and intuitive form of empathy, where individuals pick up on subtle emotional cues, energy vibrations, or even the physical sensations of others. Empaths have an innate ability to understand and non-verbally connect with the emotions of those in their purview.

Indeed, like Deanna Troid on Star Trek, Empaths literally and not figuratively feel others' emotions as a psychic ability; it is their actual superpower. It's also a lot to wield. Walking onto an elevator can feel like an emotional hall of mirrors. Empaths are a walking sonar, scanning and tracking external energies everywhere they go.

It's important to note that the concept of being an Empath has often been discussed in more spiritual or metaphysical contexts and was not considered to have a universally accepted scientific basis. This has changed in the last decade or so because of people like Dr. Judith Orloff, Harvard graduate, psychiatrist, and bestselling author, who pioneered the conversation about Empaths and their distinct profile and needs. Dr. Orloff identifies as an Empath, treats Empaths, and teaches Empaths how to navigate a world that hasn't fully understood them. Dr. Orloff, amongst others who will be highlighted here, has brought credibility to the Empath and given them a place in the human tapestry.

It took a long time for meditation and yoga to reach the mainstream as powerful and credible sources of well-being; it took scientific research and data to corroborate their robust short- and long-term effects and to pluck them from the world of woo. Now meditation and yoga are not only global human daily practices, but they also run parallel to medical prescriptions for multiple physical and psychological ailments.

Books like this one will do the same for Empaths.

Empaths and the Era of Emotions

Historically, psychological theories and psychotherapeutic work have centered around emotions, the impact of suppressing them (called "hysteria" by Freud) and learning to express them as an actual healing modality. But even

Meet The Empath

until recently, emotions remained in clinical waiting rooms, outpatient treatment settings, 12-step anonymity, and *telenovelas*. Emotions were still considered weak, reckless, soft, taboo, uncontrollable, and peripheral to everyday living and to the everyday human. Emotions were "over there," like the distant cousin that showed up at holiday dinners causing all sorts of ruckus, and although creating sometimes irrevocable scarring, they were to not be discussed again. Alcoholics Anonymous states that we are "as sick as our secrets," and I would add that we are as dis-eased as our hoarded, cluttered emotions.

The 1960s birthed geniuses, both with the last name Rogers. Fred, the sweater-and-bedroom-slippers protagonist for children's TV, and Carl, the innovative psychologist who coined the term "unconditional regard." They believed that unconditional regard for other humans and witnessing their emotions respectfully was the path to human health. I venture to say that they upgraded human civilization by emphasizing and validating human emotions as the bridge to individual psychological health and collective racial reconciliation. As transformative and ahead of their times as they were, the importance of emotional fitness still lagged behind the predominance of the mind.

The 1980s and 1990s saw the explosion of the age of information, marked by the fax, the internet, and mobile phones, amongst other technologies. The 2000s popularized the epoch of the mind—mindfulness, neuroscience, cognitive behavioral therapy were ubiquitous. Manifesting through the power of thought became big. Although prevalent in Eastern philosophies and esoteric circles for centuries, the idea that we could actually master our mind and that our mind creates our reality moved into the mainstream. And yet there remained a powerful caveat, a terrorist even, a sneaky saboteur: emotion. Underneath all of our mental mastery, positive thinking, and executive functioning is the sleeping volcano of unprocessed emotions, with alternating layers of volatility and buried potential.

Enter the era of emotions, which is marked by an increased focus on leaders and teams with high emotional intelligence. Organizations are realizing that emotional health has a direct impact on work culture and productivity.

Groups who, as a code of conduct, do not share their "dirty laundry" or who adhere to communal loyalty over their own self-care—Black, Latino, and Asian—have broken the silence and are prioritizing individual psychological health over inherited mores. Staying silent and unprocessed has borne an unsustainable high price, and the call to break ancestral chains for the next generation rings loud and clear.

This new era, prompted by the pandemic, particularly triggered Empaths all over the planet.

The emergence of Empath discussion groups and healing circles is staggering. There are so many Empaths across the globe right now, waking up, exploring their triggers, and shedding their trauma. Being triggered is, ironically, a strange rite of passage, as it is a way for Empaths to identify what aspect of intuition they have. More on this later.

The healed Empath has a big and very specific role in moving consciousness forward on this planet, and that's why there has been such a mass awakening. The healed Empath has the capacity to teach us all how to use the human emotional operating system, our human tech. The

Meet The Empath

healed Empath illustrates how to have emotional boundaries and how to have empathy without depletion.

It is the Empath who will facilitate bringing energetic awareness and spiritual practices into the world as a deterrent to unhinged fear and chaos. Their uniquely heightened capabilities—emotional regulation and calibration—are the keys to humanity's inter-relational healing.

The Empath must learn sovereignty first by disentangling themselves from their wounds and fears—and by enthroning themselves with their own gifts.

Through their own healing and embodiment, the Empath can be the "feelings-whisperer" of this new era.

I am reminded of a poem I use in all of my programs, Rumi's "The Guest House."[1]

"This being human is a guest house.
Every morning a new arrival.

A joy, a depression, a meanness,
some momentary awareness comes
As an unexpected visitor.

Welcome and entertain them all!
Even if they're a crowd of sorrows,
who violently sweep your house
empty of its furniture,
still treat each guest honorably.
He may be clearing you out
for some new delight.

The dark thought, the shame, the malice,

> *meet them at the door laughing,*
> *and invite them in.*
>
> *Be grateful for whoever comes,*
> *because each has been sent*
> *as a guide from beyond."*

Traditional Empath Characteristics

There are traditional characteristics that are the most common for Empaths. Later, I will add my own insights to these descriptors, but for now, see whether you find yourself in these pages.

The Empath needs a balance between extraversion and introversion. These labels have nothing to do with Jung's archetypes of extrovert and introvert. What's important to know here is that the Empath is actually quite good at being social and being available to people but definitely needs time to be alone and to reflect, an essential introverted quality. The Empath tends to be intense and needs time to reflect, digest, and integrate information; however, their instinct and impulse to make others feel good equally makes them adept at social situations.

The Empath feels drained by surface conversations. Can they do them? Yes. Can they network? Yes. Can they go to cocktail parties? Yes. But they prefer deep, connected conversation; conversation is one of the ways they make love. They prefer the one-on-ones where they actually get to know people. They desire to be truly seen. That's why therapy is easy for them. They also prefer smaller social groups and dinners with a core group of friends rather than huge parties. At a club, they're the ones with a small crew on the side or just with their BFF on the dance floor, jamming. Surface conversations are doable but not preferred.

The Empath attracts people who need healing. People are very attracted to the Empath because others tend to feel good about themselves in their presence. Empaths tend to be focused, emotionally available, and good listeners. People will feel safe to tell an Empath their entire story. People will open up and trust them with good reason: Empaths will be discreet, engaged, and interested—but the catch is that they might feel completely drained afterward. I call this the "sponge factor;" the Empath will absorb energy from others and their environment. Another caveat is that Empaths tend to attract the narcissist in the room because the narcissist loves a good listener and, even better, a very absorbent sponge!

Empaths struggle with boundaries and saying no. The Empath is an expert at yes! Saying no feels like they are hurting the other person. In the belief that they are hurting another, they will hurt themselves. The unhealed Empath falls on their sword often. The Empath must learn to say no, walk away, and insist on their solitude so that they can care for themselves. Saying no is self-care for the Empath.

Empaths are highly intuitive in a telepathic way. They feel things and know things, even when they don't know why or how. Yes, knowingness is an actual sixth sense that can become a skill—an ability, if you will—with time and practice.

Claudia Cauterucci

Empaths care deeply about other people, even the "bad guy." Caring is essential here and is different than loving. Empaths care about almost everything outside of themselves. Empaths have a huge heart and care about animals, the world, the elements, and random situations, amongst others. My son's description and assessment of the Empath is simple and precise: They care about the bad guy in the movie. The Empath will try to understand how they "turned bad."

Empaths are extremely affected by injustice because they care deeply about humanity. If you want to see an angry Empath, have them witness an injustice. It may be the only time you see them show up with lightning bolts. I tend to imagine the Empath with a spear in hand. The Empath stands firmly with the foot of the spear planted into the ground and the point facing toward the sky. This is the Empath saying, "Enough."

The Empath is hardwired to harmonize environments because they feel external energies in their own bodies. They impulsively strive to make others happy and believe that if they succeed, it will alleviate their own energetic discomfort. They are thus the problem-solver, the helper, the fixer, and the savior. Now this can become energetically overwhelming because everyone wants an Empath on their team. Empaths are given leadership positions everywhere because of this exact characteristic.

The Empath is popular. Even though they can be introverted in order to recharge, to integrate, and to come back to center, they are popular because of their gift of being available to others. Because the Empath is hard-wired to harmonize environments, people like them. They are fun and can be the life of the party if they feel there is tension to tame. In fact, what can be more closeted is their introverted side.

The Empath tends to override their own needs and invisibilize themselves in order to care for others. In their families, friend groups, and love relationships, they are the ones who say, "Don't worry about me. I'm good. I'm fine!" (Or insert any variation thereof.) Empaths were the child that was "fine," not causing any trouble, and may have even parented their parents.

The Empath needs to process. Period. They need to think about things and run them through their systems. They need to write and take notes, and they usually have several journals nearby for different topics. They need to think about things deeply, study them, and come back with clear answers.

The Empath is exceptionally responsible and responsive. Let me add, "over" responsible and responsive. If unhealed, this level of responsibility is compulsive and fear-driven. They will reply to late-night texts, they will work overtime, and they will go the extra mile to be responsive and responsible. This is the best babysitter, the best first-responder, the executor, the crisis manager, the store closer, and so on. This over-responsibilization is a heavy cross the Empath bears but they are highly rewarded for their unboundaried responsiveness and will thus ignore their depletion.

Empaths are innate healers. This may come as a shock. The intrinsic drive to make sure everyone is okay shows up often as the helper and caregiver. In their families, they are the ones who are filling in the spaces because they are concerned and care about what's going on, even and especially in abusive or addictive environments. People will be drawn to Empaths because their care is healing, and it soothes most environments they find themselves in.

Empaths see the elephant in the room. They are such deep feelers that energetic non-transparency shows up in their bodies like a pebble or a rock in their shoe. They require transparency because they smell the stench of unspoken tension, pain, or hostility, and it will throw them into a swirl or paralyze them. To alleviate these states, the Empath is often the one to speak to the stinky elephant and can easily be scapegoated by the group in which they find themselves.

Does any of this feel familiar to you? If so, dear Empath, it's time to put yourself—and your healing—first for a change.

Chapter 3
Three Types of Empaths

"Until you make the unconscious conscious, it will direct your life, and you will call it fate."

— Carl Gustav Jung

The Empath is not an actual clinical construct... yet. When describing them clinically, they are mostly defined within the relational construct with someone with narcissistic personality disorder (NPD) —either a parent, sibling, or lover. Narcissism may include being raised within a narcissistic culture or employed within a narcissistic corporate setting, as we'll explore later.

Whether the Empath has suffered narcissistic abuse or has been under "the reign" of a narcissist, the narcissistic paradigm serves as a petri dish for the cultivation of these Empath clinical traits. The Empath is thus studied clinically as being on the other side of the NPD coin. Following Bowlby's attachment theory, wherein the caretaker(s) who raised us becomes the relationship model we seek as adults, a narcissistic parent paves the way for a narcissistic lover because the Empath will easily default into the role originally taken with the caretaker.

Oftentimes, Empaths have difficulty referencing their own needs. When under stress, the Empath will impulsively bypass themselves for the needs of others, which lays the foundation for co-dependence and a profound identity loss. The Empath literally abandons themselves physically, mentally, emotionally, and spiritually, and because these relational models are set early in childhood, the Empath can spend most of their adult life living for others rather than themselves.

Empaths also have an energetically porous psychic structure which means that they can easily give up their own energy. This explains why they feel drained when around certain people and—if very wounded—all people. When their partner, child, parent, or boss is anxious, they will also feel anxious or drained. They are thus more sensitive to environmental insults and, clinically, to predators. For this reason, the wounded Empath is a perfect match for a narcissistic predator; the Empath will bypass themselves and bestow all their effort and energy to the narcissist, who is all too eager to exploit this gratuitous supply chain.

Lastly, Empaths have an overdeveloped inner child energy that, in its highest form, can make them fun, cute, and playful, but more often than not, translates clinically into an inner child who has not learned how to receive nourishment or support.

What this means in non-clinical language is that the Empath was forced to take care of themselves and doubtlessly, forced to care for the needs of the adult in the

Three Types of Empaths

room. Empaths often are the "parentified child" or the child who takes care of the parent, and tries to fix and solve things for them in an unconscious attempt to get their own needs met. The Empath has the wish that says, "If I take care of you (adult) and make you happy, you will feel better and eventually take care of me." It's a trickle-down relational economy, and it never works as trickle-down propositions rarely do.

The "party of one" syndrome, a phrase I coined, fits the profile of the child that survived taking care of themselves, bypassed their own needs (and probably didn't know they could have any), spent many nights ruminating on how to solve things they didn't understand, and likely were seen as high achievers because they were on overdrive as parental problem-solvers.

The "party of one" adult is anxious, hypervigilant, and often ruminates. They confuse achievement with love and are highly co-dependent or hyper-independent. As adults, the "party of one" is quite befuddling because they are incognito under the guise of high achievements and high placement in most of their endeavors. This is especially true for the Empath.

The wounded adult Empath doesn't know how to ask for protection. They may not even know they need it—and they profoundly do. They have a hypertrophied muscle to flex when others need protection, and they compulsively emerge as the first responder in most, if not all, situations. Their own needs, though, surprise them, shock them, and shame them.

Claudia Cauterucci

Two Core States

As Abdul Saad, Australian clinical psychologist from Vital Mind Coaching, explains, the Empath is psychologically confused. On the one hand, they tend to be the adult in the room because they are the expert caretaker, fixer, problem-solver, go-getter, and savior; on the other hand, they have an underdeveloped adult self, an inner child that doesn't know how to ask for protection or help. They are not able to identify their own needs and yet are always the "responsible one."

The Empath is thus oscillating between two core states. One core state is feeling very dependent on the approval, affirmation, reassurance, and acceptance of others. At its worst, this is people-pleasing because their little inner child really needs approval and love, a dependent state. They give up their energy—swap it—in the hopes that if they please others, they'll gain their protection and their support. This is the Empath in a dependent or vulnerable state.

The second state is the counter-dependent state, where the Empath denies that they're vulnerable. This can also be described as hyper-independence where they are genuinely strong, have it together, and try to function as an adult. They don't need help. They act like their inner child is fine, but predictably, and eventually, they end up collapsing again into a highly dependent state. At best, Empaths have a high rate of burnout because of this psychological whiplash; at worst, they deplete themselves into autoimmune diseases and identity erasures.

This oscillation between those two states—*I'm super strong/I got it together/Don't worry about me* to *I desper-*

ately need your approval/I need your protection/I need you to love me/Please care for me is a pseudo adulthood. The Empath was adultified while they were still a child. They live inside a Russian doll configuration wherein the smallest figurine is trapped in the public adult figure, marking the dance of hyper-vulnerability to hyper-independence.

This fluctuation results in not being able to hold their ground, often losing their position, and maybe even becoming conflict-avoidant. They relinquish their authority in order to gain protection, security, acceptance, and love—all of which they truly need because they did not receive it as a child.

Pride, Compulsive Responsiveness, and Over-Responsibility

The Empath is also over-responsibilized. This refusal to accept help from others is an Achilles' heel; it is imbued with a fragile pride. They feel ashamed of their needs because their needs were shamed as children, verbally and nonverbally. They generally feel like the lesser kid, the poor kid, and as I describe it, they experience the "little matchgirl syndrome," who, as an adult, is looking into everyone else's hearth-filled homes wondering why they don't have the same. *They crave families and a home life where they are parented.*

See how easy it might be for Empaths to fall victim to narcissistic love bombing—and how pleasing people at all costs becomes the bedrock of future adult relationships?

Claudia Cauterucci

The young Empath is seen and valued for being responsive and resilient, and those fragile and fleeting sources of pride become an identity badge.

Other adult figures, teachers, coaches, and counselors tell young Empaths they are mature and responsible; they praise those young people for staying quiet and compliant. The Empath learns to do things silently, helpfully, immediately, and alone. For the unconscious Empath, this *is* a source of pride, a gain, especially since they feel completely unseen in all the other ways they are *truly* gifted.

Consequently, and unbeknownst to themselves, they are tip-toeing on a double-edged sword. They are praised for (and left doing) many things alone for the sake of group harmony or pleasing the authority figures. This fosters a profound existential loneliness and a dysregulated attachment style that is based exclusively on self-reliance while also serving as a supply source for the needs of others.

Another critical issue is stress overload. The Empath may not know they are bypassing their own needs until they collapse; collapsing shows up as physical ailments, incapacitating migraines, fainting, severe dissociation—leaving the body—and even cancer in the long run. Highly sensitive Empaths feel attuned and absorb any environment they go into, including the state of the world. Activities like watching the news can overload their central nervous system. In the presence of narcissistic individuals, Empaths will experience severe physical symptoms and or dissociation to self-protect.

The good news—and I know we could all use some right now—is that healing for Empaths is not only possible, it's deeply powerful. If these struggles are feeling too close and too painful, pause to take a breath. I promise you, you aren't alone. Join me in looking toward the pathway to living more wholly and authentically.

The 3 Types of Empaths

Similar to how autism exists on a spectrum, Empaths, too, can be viewed as individuals varying in the intensity of their heightened sensitivity to the emotions and energies of others. Dr. Saad contends that there are three types of Empaths on this clinical spectrum who are defined by three levels of functioning—from the dysfunctional, disintegrating Empath to the high-level, high-functioning one. He characterizes these three types of Empaths as the codependent, the proud helper, and the authentic altruist.

The Codependent

The first category is the pathological, unhealthy, poor-functioning Empath, which is ***the codependent***. This Empath is usually in an abusive relationship with a narcissist.

The codependent is the person who is addicted to saving and rescuing and who feels that they are responsible for rescuing someone else out of their pathology, whether it's drug/alcohol addiction, narcissism, or other personality disorders. They exist to save this person, and this codependent has a singular focus, which is the focus of only one individual. They're not saving the world. They're not saving themselves. They are focused on saving the other. The fantasized end goal is that if the abuser/addict/personality-disordered individual is saved, they will finally have the wherewithal to love and care for the codependent. If the codependent puts enough of the work in—"ride or die, hell or high water" effort—then, finally, they will be seen, heard, and valued.

This is a very dysfunctional, toxic situation. These are the codependents who never healed from childhood trauma, most likely were raised in a disorganized attachment relationship, and were so neglected or abused that developing a sense of self outside of the relationship with the perpetrator was never an option. They are chronically in a relational cycle with a narcissist and are exploited and abused.

If Empaths do not work to process their childhood via therapy and self-reflection, the fear of abandonment will keep them trapped and beholden to exploitative relationships. At best, they will people-please, overextend, and over-responsibilize; at worst, they will find themselves with no identity at all, dissociated, and psychically sick.

The Proud Helper

The second Empath, the one in the middle of the spectrum, is average functioning and is characterized as **the proud helper**. This placement is intermediate, not pathological. It's not unhealthy, but it's showing some cracks. The proud helper likes to be seen as the "good person," the person who has a good heart, which by the way, is almost always based in truth.

The Empath has a good heart.

The caveat here is that this person has created a full identity around being the "good one with the good heart." They feel valued for being the helper, the fixer, and the savior. Without that role or that image, they feel empty. The other catch is that they view themselves as the center. Without their help, without them being the savior or the fixer, they feel that things will collapse, so the groundwork for codependent behavior and relationships is thus laid.

The proud helper Empath can be a little egocentric and engage in self-deception, swooping in on automatic without self-reflection or discernment. It is not a free act, and they don't have the insight of their internal motivation. They want to be the protagonist while secretly being resentful. But all feelings come out eventually. If unaddressed, they leak, spew, or are impulsively expelled.

This Empath can become the victim quickly and easily in their relationships, and it's usually based on truth. This Empath—like most—has suffered an abused or neglected childhood. They feel like a victim because they were one. These Empaths do not engage in the work of moving out of victimhood unless they find themselves in extreme cases—and sometimes not even then.

The Authentic Altruist

The authentic altruist has a very high level of self-awareness. The authentic altruist knows their internal motivations, knows who they are, and knows why they do things. They know their limitations and are discerning. Discernment provides them with the freedom to give or not to give. They know themselves so well that they can CHOOSE. For the authentic altruist, giving and helping is a conscious choice and not an impulsive response to chaos, crisis, or people-pleasing.

The authentic altruist realizes the best course of action usually is *not* to give help. They rely on their wisdom and understand that sometimes they don't have to help prematurely. When this type of high-functioning Empath decides to give, they're not very attached to the outcome. They're not giving so that people will notice. They are giving because they want to; their gratification is for themselves, and this shifts the locus of control from choices made for external pleasing to choices made for self-care and self-priority. The act of giving thus becomes a sovereign, free act. It is chosen.

This Empath is not upset if their attempts at helping aren't successful. They're not focused on playing the role of being the helper, the fixer, or the savior. They are not codependent or hyper-independent because they are calm enough to discern, they remain in their bodies, and they freely choose.

This Empath has had a lot of internal and somatic work, therapy, and is trauma-informed. They have learned to accept the fact that they live in the world of the non-visible, and they require attunement and comfort beyond the five senses; they need something that moves beyond the 3-dimensional, material, and visible world. This Empath will do the work to heal, plug up leakages, become more self-aware, and accept themselves.

Maybe all of us have visited versions of each of these places.

I tend to believe that if you're reading this book or if you are curious about the Empath Leader training that I facilitate, you're already on the self-healing journey. You are likely a part of the group that will do the work to be at your highest level.

And it starts with rooting back into your power.

Chapter 4
Rooted in Power

"If I could give you just two things: one is roots, and the other is wings."

— Unknown

Like Dorothy in the *Wizard of Oz*, although highly gifted and in the world of plenty, Empaths lost their way home, unaware that home was inside all along. For the Empath, the yellow brick road is a tower of energetic layers that require alignment.

The Empath's primary sensations are spiritual, if spiritual is defined as incorporeal or beyond the body. Consequently, the Empath is naturally mystical in spite of the fact that they may not have the words to describe themselves as such, just sensations. The Empath's innate ability to feel the "unseen" and to recognize energies in any setting directly corresponds with their natural connection to the spirit and the body, both forming a crucial two-pronged tuning fork for daily interactions.

Claudia Cauterucci

Spiritual authors and consciousness researchers Lester Levenson, physicist and creator of the Sedona Method, and David R. Hawkins, who wrote *The Map of Consciousness Explained*, posit in their teachings that feelings are energies that vary on a scale of decreasing density; they move from lower-level energies like shame and guilt to higher-level energies, like courage, acceptance, and love. This is compatible with the overarching Empath identity. Empaths feel, and for them, feelings are interchangeable with energy. Empaths are feeling sonars and, therefore, energy trackers.

The Chakras

In this chapter, we'll talk about being an Empath from a chakra-based perspective because chakras are defined as energy wheels or vortices that serve as power centers. If you haven't studied the chakras and you don't know much about them, the way that I tend to teach the chakras is as a visual, which presents an easier way of understanding this non-verbal, non-material familiarity.

Originating in India, chakras are a complex energy system composed of primarily seven energy whirlpools that run along the spine. Each chakra corresponds to its own distinct organs and is meant to have a sequential order. If they are misaligned, they have a striking impact on physical and emotional well-being. When chakras are aligned, a human is coherent, congruent, connected, and whole.

Wendy Da Rosa—a highly specialized Empath, healer, founder of the School of Intuitive Studies, and author of *Becoming an Empowered Empath*—provides the best and most thorough description for understanding the Empath via the chakras. At the risk of oversimplifying and not doing

Rooted in Power

Wendy's work justice, I will only focus on the first three chakras since these are the ones that cause the most suffering for the Empath.

The first chakra, the root chakra, is the foundational chakra, the flooring, per se, and like in all structures, serves to provide us with security and stability. The second and third chakras—the sacral and solar plexus, respectively—are like the engines of a ship. They are "below deck" but serve as a power source to steer forward. Without them, the Empath loses power. Due to their origin story, most Empaths have a misaligned layering of the first three chakras, and hence their sense of power in the world is skewed from the start.

The **root chakra** is of greatest importance because it is the root of all identity formation. Like a house, when the foundation is off, so is everything else. If misaligned, the structure on top, or the next identity layers, is based on an understructure that took a U-turn. The first chakra is the *seat of safety*. Another way I like to picture the root chakra is as a regal, heavy throne. For the wounded Empath, however, this throne is missing a leg. The root chakra is physically in the pelvic region.

The second chakra is the **sacral chakra,** and this chakra is all about pleasure, creativity, and sexuality; indeed, it's through our sexual urge that we become creators. Desire fuels imagination, and consistent imagination creates new worlds. When we desire, we pay attention to detail, we reach for more, we move past fear, we play, we enjoy, we are energized, and mostly, we explore. Desire propels exploration. The sacral chakra is located above the pubic bone underneath the belly button.

Claudia Cauterucci

The chakra sequence makes perfect sense within the attachment theory paradigm. When we feel safe as children and when our home foundation is stable, the child feels free to explore because it feels the presence of a securely attached parent. A securely attached child has the courage to try new things and is adventurous, knowing there is a safety net to catch them. The fearful, insecure child stays inside, maybe clinging to an attachment object, and anything new feels dangerous.

The third chakra is the **solar plexus**. The solar plexus is the will. It is our confident belief that we can move into action. Our will anchors in the self-esteem with which we navigate the world and emboldens our "I can do it" urges. Children who have multiple "I did it!" experiences present as strong and free willed because the world is their oyster. They are empowered by their sense of safety and exploratory nature. This is the truly resilient child, not because they were left alone to fend for themselves, but because they were not alone and always felt a loving caretaker in their corner. The solar plexus is located just above the navel.

The second and third chakra capture everything that's subsurface and everything between the lines in any interaction. The Empath is an expert at x-ray energetics. The Empath has the ability to experience other people's feelings, but when they are *overly empathic*—on empathy overdrive—they are *absorbing* other people's energy like an oversaturated sponge, drenched and heavy.

Misalignment: The Leaning Tower of Chakras

The Empath's origin story, starting with early childhood, is where the chakra or energetic misalignment begins. The Empath child could not get true knowledge of themselves because of an energetic overwhelm. Given their intrinsic sensitivity, the child's energetic, intuitive system is flooded.

When a child is born into an environment where they feel like they belong in their body because they feel safe and trust the people around them, the root chakra, the foundation, can safely unfurl. They can relax into who they are. The exact opposite happens to the wounded Empath child. Foundational experiences such as neglect, abuse, and having to care for the adults and/or siblings in the family system corrupt chakra alignment early on. Being left alone frequently, parenting themselves, feeling unsupported, being excluded, witnessing violence, being gay, being adopted, and any other ways of feeling extremely different from everyone else in their family produces energetic and intuitive overwhelm. The root chakra feels compromised on some level.

Other descriptors of being born into a tribe or a family structure where belonging feels untenable are being in the midst of anger torpedoes, chronic criticism and complaining, alcoholism, or even the unintentional neglect of an exhausted single parent. In these homes, the child is barraged with emotional projections and energetic landmines to manage. Focusing on discovering themselves is non-existent. Impulsively responding and dodging hostility is the name of the game.

Claudia Cauterucci

In these scenarios, the root chakra, which is at the very tailbone, is going to contract the power center for safety and trust. Like the highly sensitive Mimosa Pudica plant which closes when touched, the root chakra locks down instead of relaxing, opening, and welcoming the surrounding energies.

For little children as well as adults, safety and trust are powers. Consider the tenets of attachment theory, wherein trust and safety make the child feel exploratory, adventurous, and powerful. If we don't have a handle on that power —because instead, there is a tremendous fear about belonging and personal integration into the world—it follows that the root chakra stays protectively in contraction and closed. The foundation is not doing its job and goes askew.

Subsequently, this child's spirit will not follow the normal sequence of anchoring into safety and stability but rather will lift up higher in the body without an established foundation. The child's spirit will move into the second chakra, the sacral chakra, where creativity and sexuality reside. When the Spirit lifts higher into the second chakra, the second chakra will start to compensate by either blowing open—let's say with reckless promiscuity—or shutting down. The Empath may over-sexualize because the cascade of energetic overwhelm is skewing and tipping over.

When the Empath moves out of their emotional center in the second chakra, what happens for the intuitive or sensitive child is that they become hyper-vigilant. An internal dialogue develops that says, "It's not okay for me to have my feelings. I have to move myself aside. I have to take myself out of the equation and make other people's emotions a priority so that I know how to navigate, and so that I know how to be inside myself."

This marks the start of the Empath abandoning themselves and the development of a codependent relationship with energy and emotions. The Empath child becomes more aware and hyper-vigilant of other people's emotions around them because they feel like they do not belong in their body.

The second chakra is also the place of the mother. The Empath moves their needs out of the way, and other people sit in their mothering center. This applies to all genders since we all have female and male energies. Masculine energy is primarily expressed as assertion and outward action, and feminine energy is primarily expressed as receptivity and inwardness. (I like to think of the penile erection, standing tall, moving forward, and expressing outwardly, and the vagina, a soft, receptive, enfolding, and comforting cave as visual symbols of the energies.)

These energies are usually in flux and striving for balance, whether consciously or unconsciously. Early 20th century psychoanalyst, Carl Jung, claimed that one of the markers of psychological health is finding the balance of the masculine and feminine energies. For the wounded Empath, there is great confusion between the masculine and feminine energies, as they are continuously mothering others while also moving into action to provide, protect, and assert for the safety and well-being of our own "caretakers." Empaths are thus in a whirlwind of being both father and mother as children, and these roles rigidify if left unhealed and form the template for their adult relationships.

Claudia Cauterucci

An Empath's emotions are not their own. Their fear, anger, and grief disappear in an effort to prioritize other people's energy. Most often shaped in their childhood, this emotional-energetic reaction basically sets them up for a pattern where it is normal to create whole pathways to absorb the energies of others.

Let's move into the third chakra. The solar plexus is actually our will, and our confidence in the world, and it fuels our decision-making. When healed, Empaths decide with confidence who they are in the world. They are empowered to move into action.

In a volatile, hostile, or neglectful environment, the third chakra greatly compensates for non-grounding. For a child whose will is diminished, the search for self-esteem is a long journey ahead, full of potholes and detours. The way this child finds esteem and anchoring is by latching on—and I'm not dramatizing—to another, hook and sinker. And they do sink.

* * *

Personal share: I have a very clear example of the use of an external object as a grounding mechanism when in distress. I recall having my first EMDR treatment—eye movement desensitization and reprocessing method, a therapeutic modality—that non-verbally helps with PTSD by accessing, reshuffling, and re-interpreting a traumatic memory. The therapist invited me to ask a question I wanted answered. I was lighthearted and asked, "Why do I have extra weight on my body?" As I moved my eyes hypnotically from side to side, I didn't just remember an experience, I was directly transported to a place and time in my childhood, as if time traveling, and I could literally feel the fat on my 10-year-old body serving as a "paper weight." I had the sensation of being comforted and "weighted" down in the midst of parental chaos and absence. As I came back from the treatment, I had more compassion for the way my weight had swaddled me in a time of need.

* * *

Under the weight of the energetic onslaught, the weathered body is like the bucket, a valiant ally and instrument, caught by an invading emotional deluge, scooping and flinging energetic burdens overboard. The Empath's unconscious and tireless dance of urgency and survival persists into adulthood unless they pause to heal and realign.

For the healed Empath, coming home looks like an unfurled root chakra with lotus petals that say: "I am safe. I am stable. I am secure. I am home."

Chapter 5
Self-Care: Your Survival Kit

*"Just like moons and like suns,
With the certainty of tides,
Just like hopes springing high,
Still I'll rise."*

— Maya Angelou

Self-care is not a luxury for the Empath. It is the decisive and pivotal strategy for the Empath's healing, consequent prowess, and sovereignty.

If you are an Empath, pause and read that first paragraph again. And again.

As we've talked about, planet Earth is no joke in terms of navigation. Global events, information tsunamis, invisible energetic tornadoes, and little-to-zero training in operating our human technology—particularly our emotional regulation and calibration—humans are left awkwardly walking around as if blindfolded, arms flailing forward, trying to

Self-Care: Your Survival Kit

discern their path and inevitably bumping, or rather, crashing into other humans.

In a world that can feel chaotic and disorganized, with torrents of information and narcissists skulking about, it's no wonder that the Empath is constantly in a dissociated state or what I describe as "leaving the body."

Dissociation is a part of the human operating system that allows us to cope and defend against highly stressful, often dangerous situations that our psyche cannot understand, bear, or tolerate. Examples of these unbearable states are sexual, physical, and emotional abuse, war, and chaotic environments. Imagine being a raw, exposed, and unconfined walking sensor, picking up on every single vibration surrounding them. To survive, the untrained Empath either lives in a dissociated state or compulsively endeavors to harmonize their environment until driven to the ground—or both. Either way, the Empath does not self-care and often does not know who they truly are. Their identity is wrapped up in how they serve others.

Self-care is the way home.

Self-Care Specifics

Let's talk about very specific ways that the Empath can practice self-care. I'm going to start with Dr. Judith Orloff, who I describe as the Queen Empath because she not only put the word "Empath" smack into the mainstream as a Harvard grad and psychiatrist, but she staked a credible place for the Empath by establishing specific psychological and emotional protocols for their well-being.

Claudia Cauterucci

Dr. Orloff was born a highly sensitive Empath, or an HSP, whose susceptibilities go beyond just energies but also include sounds, textures, and images. Like most Empaths, she had psychic abilities as a child, which were dismissed by her parents. She felt weirder and weirder and stranger and stranger as a child. Feeling "weird" is a consistent and constant experience for the Empath yet imbued in "weird" are actual skills and abilities, like sensing and understanding things that weren't being said.

As a child, Dr. Orloff opted to get quieter. In her teenage years, she self-medicated with drugs and alcohol to suppress her abilities and her sensitivities. As a young adult, she was determined to fit into the establishment and went to Harvard Medical School, dodging its own narcissistic system, which at the time was rife with hostile competitive rankings and dangerous academic overdrive. What kept her going was her commitment to proving that she could succeed in this world. She knew that if she had all of the credentials—in this case, at the highest level, graduating from Harvard Medical School—she could start sharing about being a highly sensitive Empath, thus silencing, if not circumventing, people who saw her as "woo."

Accumulating decades of data not only from herself but from the patients she treated, Dr. Orloff wrote the book *The Empath's Survival Guide*. It's a manual that provides self-care routines and techniques that have really worked for her. I see it as a manifesto that puts Empaths on the map! She describes how Empaths get anxious, drained, tired, and depressed, and the world feels like too much; unbeknownst to them, they are depleted Empaths.

Self-Care: Your Survival Kit

Dr. Orloff states that Empaths are consistently misdiagnosed by conventional medicine and are thus overmedicated. Because of their sensitivity, Empaths actually require lower doses of medication, but given their symptomatology, they are prescribed very high doses. Empaths end up having panic attacks or worse because the world feels like a place of complete disarray.

In her book, *Are You an Empath?*, she states that Empaths don't need medication and genuinely don't want medication because they can, and need to, *soothe and heal themselves from the inside out*. Oh, no words ring more true! So much of the Empath experience is from the inside out—what I call the inner journey. This book boldly claims that the Empath navigates the external world through their internal compass, which further emphasizes the insistence on self-care.

If you're an Empath struggling to make time for self-care, let me reiterate that it is not a luxury. It must be a priority—for you and for the sake of a world waiting for you to fully realize your superpowers.

I'll relate the following thirteen Empath self-care principles directly to you (and me, because we are together in this). I hope you'll take them to heart and bring them to life in your everyday routines.

1. The Empath needs alone time.

We need time to reflect and to integrate. The Empath does not have the same filters as others, so places like crowds, malls, concerts, and family reunions can feel overwhelming if we haven't prepared. We also need alone time to organize and file away our day, accommodating our external experiences into their place internally. This helps us settle into a safe and stable root chakra, a wellspring of exquisite wisdom.

2. The Empath must express their needs authentically.

Dr. Orloff proposes that there can be too much togetherness in a relationship. If your partner wants to spend all their time with you, you can gently mark boundaries, not as rejections, but rather as your time to integrate all the information that you've been taking in - energetic and emotional information. Alone time is a time for decompression and integration. If explained as such, it does not have to be viewed as a rejection.

* * *

Personal share: My father was an introvert, but he was in a highly visible career that demanded a great deal of social interaction. When he came home, my mother always rushed us away and hushed us to "not bother Daddy," not uncommon for most homes in the 1970s. Because neither of them knew or understood to describe it as a time for decompressing, those memories were lodged in me as a consistent abandonment wounding. Today we know better.

* * *

3. The Empath needs to develop their throat chakra.

In layspeak, we Empaths must learn how to communicate directly. We render ourselves mute because we don't want to hurt feelings. We misconstrue boundaries as rejections and fear hostility when placing them. We project our own abandonment fear, so boundaries, in our mind, become an opportunity to leave or be left. We must learn to speak directly about what we need, in kindness. There is an Empath-way, and it's kindness. We must also slowly accrue data that there are humans who won't punish us or leave us when we have needs. Speaking to our needs helps us survive; hence, all forthcoming relationships must be based on discussions around needs, wants, and preferences. I recommend sooner rather than later as it is a litmus test for how the relationship will unfold.

4. **The Empath needs to ground**.

Just as electricity grounds in the earth, we Empaths draw back our energetic field from others by grounding. We experience sensory overload in the form of panic attacks and anxiety that can come on very quickly. Dr. Orloff suggests honoring them, and I couldn't agree with her more. I see panics, depression, and anxieties as messages. Our body is trying to get our attention. Listen. If available, it's helpful to listen with a guide or with a therapist so you are not afraid as the feelings move through your body and you learn to understand their messages.

I encourage my folks to actually ground by sitting or lying on the floor; this provides both the physical sense of safety and the metaphorical image of safeguarding the root chakra. It is no wonder that so many spiritual traditions, if not all of them, invite us to kneel or sit on the ground.

Dr. Orloff suggests that when you feel your anxiety coming on, excuse yourself and go to a bathroom. For those of you who have taken the Dynamic Meditation Method with me, I proclaim that cars and bathrooms are our churches!

Whether you are smack in the middle of a happy hour or in a staff meeting, go into a public bathroom stall and use your tools. Dr. Orloff has a three-minute meditation, where you put your hand on your heart—embodiment—and focus on something you love for three minutes. Breathe, calm your central nervous system, place your hand over your heart, and ground yourself by touching your body.

I recommend using Dynamic tools, where we either "say yes" to breathe out the emotions filling us or we ask about which survival program is consuming us at the moment (wanting safety, wanting control, or wanting approval). Actual grounding meditations for moments when we are alone are quite powerful because they are gentle and structured. My toolkit includes one, and Wendy da Rosa has a very good one as well.

5. The Empath must practice self-compassion.

Self-compassion is non-negotiable. The Empath leaves themselves out of most relational equations. They are experts in having compassion for others and seeing everyone else's point of view (a leadership skill when honed), but they lack self-compassion. As new Earth philosopher and YouTube influencer, Amanda Flaker emphasizes, the Empath removes themselves from the relational equation. To thrive, we must include ourselves. In wounded Empath math, one (usually the narcissistic variable) plus zero (the serving Empath) equals only one. When we insert ourselves as relevant, worthy, substantial, and powerful, we SHOW UP as the second variable in the equation, tallying two.

We matter, and as this book will show you, we matter more than you can imagine.

6. The Empath must love their inner child.

Speaking to and loving our inner child is helpful because it was when we were children that things began to go astray. You can tell your inner child to find a safe place. You are the first in line to protect and to defend when there's sensory overload. It also merges the Russian dolls wherein you are both the competent adult who can hack pretty much anything, as well as the scared child who needs witness and encouragement.

Using the phrase "I am both this and that" bolsters self-esteem and self-acceptance. It heals dissociated imposter syndrome that perpetuates serving the wrong people.

* * *

Personal share: I had a complicated surgery, and I was afraid to do my own self-care. When I pictured my inner child, I had the courage to do it because it was the inner child that was afraid. The adult in me kept saying, "You've got this. You're doing great. Look at you doing this!" My inner child was afraid to take care of my scary wound but, the adult me talked her through it and compassionately self-cared.

* * *

As a human and as a humanity, we are meant to be both this and that, we are allowed to be both genius and imperfect, we must keep the child-like wonder and admire the ferocious, fully grown adult.

7. The Empath must learn to say no.

Although this feels connected to finding your throat chakra, saying "No!" is intentionally more specific and does not include defending or over-explaining. No is no. We're great at saying yes, and that makes us amazing in the world. We're willing. We're eager. We're excited. We help. We raise our hand first. In my Dynamic Meditation Method, saying yes is an actual tool for releasing emotions, and willingness is considered a courageous and highly meditative state. But since we are navigating a three-dimensional reality called planet Earth, where there are multiple creatures co-existing and forces that do engage in unbalanced domination, saying no is a spear we can resolutely thrust into the ground without attacking.

Listen to your tiredness. Listen to your "want to be alone." Notice those creepy crawlies in someone's presence. Notice when someone is unilaterally talking or droning on. Notice and say "No!" internally or externally. Decide to develop this muscle.

8. The Empath must create daily rituals, or as I call them, RICHuals, that calm the central nervous system (CNS).

Our CNS is our CVS—our emotions are chemicals flooding our body. Just as we stress and shower in cortisol, we can bathe our CNS with soothing, comforting waves of endorphins, oxytocin, and serotonin. These rituals can be simple and provide a committed routine that underscores self-love as an intention. Light candles when working or cooking; elongate your water experiences like showers and baths, even if by five minutes; have music on with a little speaker in your bathroom on your desk or in the kitchen; if you are close to animals, touch them, walk

Self-Care: Your Survival Kit

them, smell them, have your heart be filled by them consciously.

9. The Empath must stop rushing.

Stop rushing—it is a disguised form of fawning. For Empaths, rushing triggers survival reactions like feeling scared, being punished, unconscious hyperventilating, and what I call the "I'm so sorry" state, which is an ingrained sense of profound fear-based inadequacy. Don't be fooled, even when rushing gets you there faster, it mostly makes you leave your body. For people with high anxiety or recovering from PTSD or healing from narcissistic abuse, rushing is a survival, dissociative state. For the rushing parent, it creates an anxious environment for your children and embeds rushing into their bodies.

Do anything to stop rushing. Give yourself more time to move slowly and meticulously. Mindfully notice when you rush, stop, and settle back into your body by breathing into the root chakra.

10. The Empath must connect with nature in any way possible.

Empaths have struggled to belong in their families and the world at large. Time in, and with, nature can be a surprisingly enormous healing resource. It provides us with a sensation of unconditional, non-judgmental belonging. We don't have to defend anything or to be something we are not. Nick Werber, an integrative coach who specializes in family constellations, with an emphasis on the black sheep in the family, says it best, "Nature not only holds as we are, WE ARE NATURE. We are not something separate and it doesn't take much time for our minds and bodies to settle back into that knowing." Werber claims that this is why those who have felt like outsiders in their family or cultural systems, have such a strong reaction to the destruction of nature: It is reminiscent of "a destructive authority who is gatekeeping and disconnecting us from a sense of belonging, and that storyline runs very deep."

Even if you're in a city and even if you grew up without being exposed to nature, like I was, you can learn how to connect with nature in small ways, like nurturing plants.

* * *

Personal share: I water my plants slowly and carefully and praise them for their expressive growth. I combine listening to gentle music or a spiritual podcast, walking my fur creature, and getting outside a few times a day. I am intentional about looking up as I walk to see the expanse of the sky and to receive the sun. I do all my gratitudes to the universe, to God, to source, as I walk.

* * *

11. The Empath must embody.

For most humans, the body is the reservoir of accumulated energy. Feelings are energetic pods. Unless we detangle, declutter, and decompress them, they will inevitably amass, leak, drizzle, protrude, and implode somewhere inside our body. Knowing how to psychologically untie these multilayered, festering energetic knots is essential because, over time, they become stubborn squatters camping out in our lungs, gut, and lower back. They cluster into rogue cells and rot into disease.

Self-Care: Your Survival Kit

If the Empath stays in chaotic and hostile environments, they will self-protect by forming a moat of fat around themselves (common for abused children), losing inordinate weight to become invisible, disassociating into a zombie-like appearance where they are mute and their gaze is hollow, succumbing to auto-immune diseases, or committing suicide. I have treated all of these versions, and if you've watched any documentaries on cults or narcissistic abuse, you can track this progression of disembodiment.

The Empath must proactively find their path back to living inside their bodies by doing vigorous psychological work paired with any form of bodywork that helps them be in their bodies again. Somatic releasing through the hips, yoga, hot yoga, breath work, and lymphatic massage are amongst some that are particularly beneficial for trauma. Dancing, roller skating, swimming, and laughing are other ways of coming back into the body.

The Empath who knows how to come back into their body is what I call the enthroned Empath, who understands that sitting inside themselves culminates their healing. Intentional embodiment is graduation.

12. The Empath must connect rather than attach.

Dr. Judith Orloff underscores the difference between connection versus attachment. In the characteristics listed earlier in the book, I specified the Empath's profound urge to connect. We need to feel *connected* to the Self and to others. If we just attach to another, which we tend to do when unhealed, but are not deeply connected, it can be draining. Think of spouses or maybe someone you help or people in the extended family. You may be attached to them, but you don't feel connected to them. This may answer why you feel unsatisfied or depleted. In your private spaces, like your home, deep connection is a form of self-care. Do not settle for less. If you can't shift your living arrangements, make sure you find time to deeply connect with yourself.

13. The Empath must be ferocious about their energy needs.

Energy is our fuel source and our currency. Be a good steward: Treasure your energy and protect it. For people who are in the public eye, run retreats, work with groups of people, or attend conferences, make sure you have time alone in your hotel room. Have a meditation on hand. Make sure you get to sleep. Make sure you know when you can't talk anymore. If you're going to conferences, if you're with your family all day long, or if you are a caregiver, protect your time by scheduling a slot for yourself and using your psycho-spiritual toolkit.

These are non-negotiables. Self-care is our empowerment and elixir. Your ferocity about your energy will become a bodyguard that helps you be in the world.

***

Personal share: For some Empaths like me, group chats can be quite overwhelming, and they activate my compulsive need to respond. I have a group of neighbors who put me on a group chat. One of the neighbors kept informing us about cars that were being stolen in the neighborhood, dogs that were lost, etc. I don't subscribe to any of the neighborhood watch apps because it overwhelms me and produces anxiety in me. She also kept texting about the news on the group chat. I mustered my ferocious courage, and combined aligned approaches in a request: First, I honored my need to be respectful and kind as an Empath, and said, "Thank you so much for looking out for us...I really appreciate it;" second, I was authentic and revealed that I had actually unsubscribed from the neighborhood watch feeds because it made me anxious; third, I expressed that it was important for me to belong and shared my appreciation for being a part of the group chat for fun stuff and get-togethers; and lastly, I marked a boundary and requested to be taken off the chat but respected their sovereignty in sharing anything they wanted to continue sharing. She and everyone else were quite kind back and continued to invite me to neighborhood events. I knew that I would have sensory overload if I was being told every danger in the neighborhood. That was a way for me to say no kindly.

* * *

I feel like these words from Derek Walcott's, *Love After Love*, poem was an encouragement to the Empath.[1]

"The time will come
when, with elation
you will greet yourself arriving
at your own door, in your own mirror
and each will smile at the other's welcome,
...Give back your heart
to itself, to the stranger who has loved you
all your life, whom you ignored
for another, who knows you by heart.
...Sit. Feast on your life."

Claudia Cauterucci

For the Empath—and I mean this in the most loving way possible—I hope the message is abundantly clear: Learn what your needs are and take care of them.

Also, things are about to get weird, in the most wonderful way. Check this out...

Chapter 6
What Kind of Psychic Are You?

*"We were born before the wind, also younger than the sun...
let your soul and spirit fly, into the mystic."*

— Van Morrison

Psychic, Say What?!

Before you balk at the word psychic, let's get some definitions of psychic out of the way so you understand what I am describing and how I'm using it.

As Oxford defines it:

1. relating to or denoting faculties or phenomena that are apparently inexplicable by natural laws, especially involving telepathy or clairvoyance.
2. relating to the soul or mind

Cambridge describes a psychic person as one who "has a special mental ability."[1]

Claudia Cauterucci

In psychoanalytic theory, which is my foundational training, psychic denotes our mental processes, particularly those involving the dance between conscious and unconscious experiences and behaviors. Studying the unconscious determinants of our behavior, in my view, allows us to understand and strengthen the bridge between our internal world and its effects on our external world.

In straight talk, psychic, for me, means everything that feels real, is invisible, and throws signs of its existence into the material world to see if it will stick, like spaghetti on a wall. As far as I'm concerned, at minimum, it behooves us to stay curious and study these phenomena; at maximum, it provides us with a sublime, sensual, life-enriching tango with the divine source of all-that-is.

I am relieved to join a roster of exciting and interesting philosophers, quantum physicists, neuroscientists, spiritual leaders, mystics, and walkers of *El Camino de Santiago* in this belief. They are doing the courageous and hard work of corroborating this divine relational commitment between the unseen and the seen and how it enhances our life on planet Earth.

The belief that psychic phenomena—gestated internally and emitted as the electromagnetic fields that surround all humans—is a verifiable and foundational source for relational configurations, power dynamics, and human potentialities has libraries of data, both scientific and by centuries of word of mouth. Our psychic dialogue is the fine print to all religious, political, cultural, and societal brawn, and leaving it buried in the ancient hallways of woo, fantasy, or wizardry is reckless. History has shown us that the "unspokens" brewing, festering, and amassing in the dark create an

What Kind of Psychic Are You?

energetic field that can literally overthrow us, molest our babies from right under our nose, and barge into government hallways to dictate national policy.

Psychic dominance, not logic, is central to mob mentality. It enslaved, tortured, and massacred millions based on abstractions such as forehead size and skin color. The hiss of unruly psychic indulgence has exploited children and all those on the outskirts of society seeking to belong. Do not let the invisibility of the human psychic discourse fool you; it fills our social media, our primaries, our traffic lanes, our parenting, and our waiting in line at the dry cleaning.

Our First Language

Where does it begin? All humans are born with intuitive and psychic abilities. It is our first language. When the fetus is floating in the water of the umbilical sac, it is absorbing information from the mother and the environment through the sac. Communication *is* happening in real-time. Intentional seeing, hearing, or talking come later and are, in fact, a secondary level of communication. Both are equally essential to human existence, but one is disregarded after the birth canal.

Think of it this way: In marketing, the words, images, colors, and sounds (the visible) are the clothing draped over the psychic messaging, which is "How do I allure, seduce, request, and inform you so that you become attracted to me....so that you love me?" The use of the five external senses is stage two to strategic marketing as well as to being human. Stage one is the non-verbal, energetic concoction that happens inside the human and then radiates outward.

Claudia Cauterucci

Unfortunately, and often because we lack training in our "humanness," once the child is born, our psychic intuitive senses fade into the background. We are not taught to acknowledge unspoken messages while being engulfed in them. No fault to the parents who likely were also not taught to validate the unspoken psychic energies filling up the relational household ... but are subjugated by them. We all know when mommy is sad, tense, or mad, even if she doesn't say anything. We know when daddy wants to be left alone even when he's not asking. We know what it's like when an adult's presence projects something other than care. Words like "creepy," "weird," "uncomfortable," and even "scary" supplant the psychic energetic code and are left floating without follow-up or corroboration because they are logically indescribable and therefore deemed irrelevant. By the way, this is the narcissist's or the perpetrator's expertise: manipulating psychic energy while grooming in physical and material seduction.

Institutions such as Hollywood, the Catholic Church, and our political landscape, amongst many, are rife with the land mines of the psychic unspoken. The "Me Too" movement, rampant public disclosure of pedophilia, and documentaries on cult tactics, including within political systems, are these psychic unspokens exploding, but mostly as an aftershock or hangover of the torrents of energetic manipulation that preceded them.

When we backtrack and connect the dots, we realize there were all sorts of psychic warning signs: the feeling that something (or someone) is odd, the hair raising on the back of the neck, the raised eyebrows at something not overly inappropriate but just enough, the silent and self-censored shocks, the creepy crawlies ... all were there! Something felt "off," but the *sliver of truth* behind which it hides, combined with the fear of group ostracism and deep un-belonging—typical of cult tactics, gangs, and abusive homes—tipped the scales just enough to abort any questioning, even within the self.

How many times do we study 1930s Europe and trace the slow rise of the tidal wave that was coming? The warnings were all there, but as in most cases of impoverished subjugation, we just didn't know how to read. Humans have been psychically illiterate, and those who have proclaimed that "the emperor has no clothes" have metaphorically and physically been burnt at the stake, branded as a loon, sent to the guillotine, or told to "just relax."

The secondary dialogue of the five senses trumps the psychic subtitles, and we are paying a large, in some cases irrevocable, price for our energetic illiteracy. Hence, THIS BOOK. This intentional backdrop puts the need for the "Leader" in "Empath Leader." This book unapologetically invites you to master the language of psychic energy for the healing of our internal and communal existence. We are not playing around. Notice I didn't say "learn" the language. You have the language, you know the language, you just dismiss the language. We are here to master it.

"A priori" Senses

Psychic language is real, the invisible is powerful, and it's time to learn to read. Why haven't we?

After birth, the incarnated, material existence takes precedence over the spiritual/energetic/psychic/unseen (I use these interchangeably) conversation that surrounds us at all times. This makes sense given that, as Madonna sings, we do live in a material world. Our incarnation distracts us completely, and yet the body is the antenna that feeds us all the information coming from the unseen. It is not an overstatement to claim that we took a huge U-turn at birth by believing that the body is here all by itself, disconnected from its source. It is actually the connector to Source, the message center, the charging station, the interpreter, and the bridge to other humans.

We got so derailed as organized religions taught us to hate our bodies, pulled the plug from the unseen, and constructed an upside-down funnel where only a few had "the powers." Dividing and conquering became the language over God, over nature, over creatures, and over other humans. Our personal and intimate relationship to the sublime unseen got ripped from our arms, and humans were ridiculed or punished for claiming a unilateral connection with it.

Our noble and logical focus becomes the mastery of verbal language, and indeed, it is a sensible, pleasurable, creative, and knowledge-inducing tool that connects and expands us. The more languages we know, the more connected we are to each other and to our prowess. The distortion is relegating the spiritual/energetic/psychic world and its language to a dusty box in the attic. As par for the course, spiritual and energetic resurgences startle us, scare us, and make us doubt ourselves, so we stuff them back into the box or into a Halloween horror movie, unexplored and disenfranchised.

If acquainted with Carl Jung's psychoanalytic work, these disenfranchised parts of ourselves and of our collective humanity form into "the shadow." Like in our personal lives, humanity has hidden, handcuffed, punished, demeaned, and destroyed its shadow side out of sheer fear of the unknown ... or of the unexplained powerful.

The shadow thus stalks and torments us—it is needy, clingy, and demanding until we provide it with care and attention. As in most cases, validation makes it less spastic. Once acknowledged and integrated, the promise is that we become more whole in self-acceptance, moles and all. As a whole human (or as a whole humanity), we are no longer afraid of ourselves and can release our defensive, paranoid, even attacking stance, vis á vis our life experience. Human beauty and human imperfection co-create our psychic balance.

We are not taught or trained to use this human technology to which we are all privy. In the past, these were called extrasensory perceptions, or ESP. This book contends that they are not extra at all, but in actuality, they are "a priori" original senses.

Physical senses are a toolkit for incarnated living with which we touch, swaddle, see, gaze, hear, taste, procreate, and protect. As on any road trip, they are a powerful and delightful navigating system. They are, however, limited in their scope.

Touch reaches as far as we can extend our hand. Smell, speaking, and hearing also have a limited radius. FaceTime and T-Mobile serve as "extra" technology, a booster seat of sorts, to our physical human tech.

Our intuitive senses, or our psychic tech, are not limited to materiality, distance, time, or space. Although a voracious

Claudia Cauterucci

fan of quantum physics, I am no expert, so allow me to baby-talk some of what I know. Quantum entanglement is indeed a complex phenomenon, but simply put, quantum entanglement is a theory that posits that communication requires an exchange of data and that quantum entanglement occurs when two particles are inextricably linked together, no matter their separation from one another.

Scientists explain that quantum entanglement describes how multiple particles can be linked together in a way, such that the measurement of one particle's quantum state determines the possible quantum states of the other particles. This connection does not depend on the location of the particles in space. Even when entangled particles are separated by inches or lightyears, changing one particle will make a change in the other. "Even though quantum entanglement appears to transmit information instantaneously," writes mathematician and physicist Andrew Zimmerman Jones of Wabash College, "it doesn't actually violate the classical speed of light because there's no 'movement' through space."[3] The bottom line is that no matter where you are, you can return to your spiritual source in an instant.

We are indeed connected to all humans and things, seen and unseen. Thanks to the invisible quantum threads that make us one pulsating organism, distance and gravity are inconsequential for us to repel or attract anything through energetic focus alone. We can message people who are not in front of us. We can view remotely. We can sense an upcoming event. We can feel and translate the energies surrounding us. We can get the unpredictable impulse to call someone who is in need. Like a strong pitching arm or a backstroke, with effortful concentration and practice, we can harness, fine-tune, and increase the reach and power of our psychic knowledge.

Human Tech

Our mind is like a computer. Our left hemisphere processes facts, planning, and organization. Although these left-brain functions are responsible for most of our daily living, it resembles having a computer that's not connected to the internet. It receives input and has limitations. That's who we are if we only exist through our physical senses. When we exist with our physical, intuitive, and psychic senses, it's like the computer is then attached to a modem. That modem can then connect to the internet and gain endless knowledge. The right hemisphere of our brain, which is the creative part that doesn't function solely on time, space, and facts, is the part of our brain that is artistic. It opens, gets downloads, and receives "out-of-the-blue" messages. It's the musical part, as in the case of Mozart and Beethoven, who could hear and see the notes of their compositions before writing them.

Amanda Flaker was the first person I heard use the phrase "human tech." She described, rather exalted, the astounding psychic human capacity and circumference as an energetic force that dominates all human interactions. Our human tech is our human internet: an invisible web that connects us to all-that-is, all-that-was, all-that-will-be, and each other.

The internet is based on humanity's psychic abilities; in other words, our ability to reach across space and time and transfer data without speaking or writing. Humanity has chronicled, since the beginning of all time, our ability to receive messages through dreams, through auditory messaging, through images, through visions, and this is recorded. Ancient religious texts and CIA files are replete with examples.

Human technology is the 1.0 version of the internet and of artificial intelligence. Fear not, it all starts with us, and once we learn to appreciate it, collaborate, and learn from it, it will end with us...US being HUMANITY.

It's humanity that's being imitated! Go figure.

A parallel and powerful narrative can be found with the people who were crucified, executed, and burned at the stake for these exact abilities. The Dark Ages—which I believe ended with the birth of this millennium and began to show its cracks circa 2012—degraded psychic natures and high intuition to something of the occult. No wonder it's been terrifying to be human, not just in our imperfection, but in our perfection.

I am not oblivious to the fact that I am a psychotherapist and that my whole career is pillared by the American Psychological Association and the research-driven Diagnostic Statistical Manual. Its distinct diagnostic categories include visual, auditory, and paranoid hallucinations as possible disordered symptoms and germinations of psychopathic disorders. These are cases—and yes, there are many —of human technology going rogue and unharnessed, like a cancer cell that, because of dismissal, disregard, or inattention, was not caught early and taken seriously and consequently became destructive. Outlier cells left alone and misunderstood can storm our hallways on a killing spree for sure, whether inside our body or out in the world. All the more reason to study and understand human psychic phenomena so that more of us don't feel so alone or "crazy."

What Kind of Psychic Are You?

When something goes wrong, something is wrong...but it doesn't have to turn bad. We need to know the symptoms (the group of facts signaling a disease) and their subsequent diagnosis to guide us in the study of the symptomology (the study of these symptoms). Study is what therapists, medical providers, historians, scientists, philosophers, and healers do to help humanity. It is to our individual and collective benefit to study the psychic human technology that we all have and in which we can train.

Study is a path to healing. The Empath loves to study.

The Basics

Let's just start with the basics. We are hardwired with our psychic senses and our physical senses. Children are absorbing both energetic and concrete information at lightning speed. The first three years, in the laying down of the first three foundational chakras, are paramount in determining whether the glitches in our hardware will cause serious challenges down the line.

"Give me a child until he is 7, and I'll show you the man," Aristotle asserted.[2] The human child is introjecting—a psychological word that basically means "swallowing whole" without digestion or discernment— all of the seen and unseen information surrounding them from their caregivers, culture, ethnicity, society, schooling, and religion. Bowlby's attachment theory, for example, is an amalgam of relational actions, behaviors, and energies that is interpreted by the child through their intuitive and physical technology that later becomes their blueprint for adult relationships. At first, adult relationships are not based on what we want or even what we dream of, but rather, on the unconscious handbook our ancestral family of origin gave us.

Basically: We are formed and molded by the seen and unseen energies into which we are born. *Punto.*

If you haven't picked up on it yet, I am here to tell you, dear Empath, that we are born and hardwired with the abilities not only to absorb unseen energies, but also to distinguish them, tame them, and train them into our superpower.

You have non-verbally known this your entire life. You are officially validated!

What is Intuition?

Knowing that we are intuitive creatures is important, especially as Empaths, because it is very likely that throughout our whole lives, we've received messages or intuitive hits that we had no idea how to handle or translate into action. Having this knowledge helps us feel less weird, less ungrounded, and even less "crazy," and, for Empaths, it is the first step towards acknowledging our prowess and acquiring sovereignty. By integrating this core aspect of ourselves, we are less subject to its chaotic attention-seeking. Other ways to describe these intuitive messages are a sixth sense, spidey sense, hits, downloads, or "a coming through."

My favorite definition of intuition comes from Wendy DaRosa. In her book *Becoming an Empowered Empath*, she describes intuition as a "conscious awareness communicating through the human experience." Some of us might call it our soul, inner voice, higher wisdom, higher self, higher mind, higher power, God, guides, or angelic frequen-

What Kind of Psychic Are You?

cies. It's when we are in union with the Divine, or if you're not spiritual, with the quantum field. It is the experience that we are in communion with a consciousness that is higher or grander than us.

Energy and emotional healing are a huge part of developing our intuition. Healing our power centers first—the root chakra, sacral chakra, and solar plexus—is absolutely required for us to really be enthroned and embodied and able to hear, validate, and respect our inner wisdom, soul, or higher self.

There are four aspects of intuition:

1. Clairsentience, our feeling sense: We feel things.
2. Claircognizance, our knowing sense: We know something even when we don't know how we know it.
3. Clairaudience, our silent hearing sense: We actually hear messaging without spoken words.
4. Clairvoyance, our seeing the unseen sense: We see a vision, an image imbued with meaning, a word, or a quote that no other can see.

These "Clairs" give us meaningful information and can show up at any time, in daylight, in conversation, in meditation, and often in dreams. Once your Clairs are understood, tracked, studied, and harnessed, you will have a better idea of how and when they come through.

A full circle here: These four aspects of intuition are related to our power centers or our chakras. When we don't have access to these four aspects of intuition, it's because, in some ways, our chakras are still blocked and misaligned.

Claudia Cauterucci

The Clairs

If you speak the language of spirituality, it's your soul or divine self that's trying to communicate with you. If you're not and prefer the language of science, this is the way that human beings are hardwired to use our electromagnetic fields to communicate with each other, animals, or nature. Either way, the point is that there is massive knowledge, wisdom, and warning available to us if we just get our wounded perceptual field out of the way. We are in constant communication with the quantum field and can learn how to intentionally interact with it.

Let's get to know the Clairs.

Are you clairsentient? These are the feelers, people who walk into a room and non-verbally feel what's happening. You feel the mood, and the energetic tone, and you feel the energy of others. If you are connected to yourself, you can distinguish and feel the emotions of others and not confuse them with being yours. You can feel the subtleties, what I call, the psychic subtitles. You can also feel the deeper need in the room.

Beware: Because you can feel what needs to happen in a group, in a situation, or in a room, if unhealed, you may compulsively respond to the need, whether asked or not. If you remain wounded and thus, undiscerning, you will try to solve, fix, and save, and you will do it well, but for the high price of your own depletion.

Are you claircognizant? This is a knowing sense. It's kinesthetic in nature, which means that you are in tune with energies around an object, like a body.

What Kind of Psychic Are You?

If you're the person who says, "I don't know how, but I know," you're likely claircognizant. Claircognizance can show up as a sudden stomach ache or headache, it can show up as chills or goosebumps, and if you mindfully notice what is being spoken at the time or what you are seeing, you are "in knowing" that you are receiving a message—it feels like a complete alignment.

Individuals with claircognizance can receive their messaging when they are on a walk or in the shower. Moving the body mindfully can invite the knowingness to come through. Our inner child is another messenger. Just as children know so many things intuitively, so does our inner child. Listen to the "knowing" through the lens of the inner child, and again, it may feel like, "I don't know why I know this, but I really know this."

Are you clairaudient? This is the ability to hear the higher self, to hear your heart. It is not exactly sounds or an auditory hallucination—although some people can hear their guides, angels, or God through words or songs—it is a message in a silent hearing form. If you break down the word, it means "clear hearing," and it's the clarity that provides the wisdom.

Clairaudience does not feel like your own voice. It distinctly "sounds" like an objective voice, without judgment, opinion, or feeling. It is strikingly nonpartisan, which gives it more credibility. Even the words it uses may be unlike the words you would use. People who have channeled books, like *A Course in Miracles*, *Conversations with God*, *The Seth Material*, or even the Christian Gospels, have described *receiving* the content and knowing for certain that it did not come from their personality or ego selves.

Claudia Cauterucci

Are you clairvoyant? These are the folks who have visions. Their higher knowledge comes to them in pictures or images or a higher perspective. A clairvoyant can see the vision when no one else can. I call this their X-ray vision. In some cases, these people—these visionaries—can see the task at hand, its problems, its solutions, and its timeline. Others have actual visions, dreams, or predictions in the form of images.

Clairvoyance has been interchangeable with predictive abilities. I hold that there are many clairvoyant humans who have an extraordinary capacity to see and understand the ordinary. Individuals who actually "see" solutions to mathematical equations, "see" others' electromagnetic fields in colors, "see" internal issues through external factors, not because they have studied math, or auras, or body language, but because they organically "see" invisible constructs. In most cases, these individuals are called geniuses, and they are, *and* it's because of their feelingness, knowingness, and seeingness.

When it comes to the Clairs, you may have several. Some of you might be blocked in a few, and some of you might be flowing with all four. Each of us can train for all of them, but be stronger or natural in one or two. It is important to study all of them and fine-tune yourself to the one(s) you choose.

- Clairvoyance starts in the third eye or the crown, because that's where we get our visions.
- Clairaudience is connected to the throat chakra because it's connected to the ear, nose, and mouth.

What Kind of Psychic Are You?

- Claircognizance is the back body and the heart because of an overall sense of knowingness.
- Clairsentience is the second and third chakra, the feeling, passion, and subtlety chakras.

The root chakra grounds them all. That's why it's so important for us to really feel clean and healed in our root chakra because look at all the work that it does for all the rest of them.

This may all feel weird, strange, or right on the money! Am I speaking your exact language? The language of energy, feelingness, knowingness, seeingness, and hearingness. You may feel like, many of us, you've known this your entire life and had no words for it. If this is the case, trust that your empowerment is coming and coming BIG, like globally big.

In the meantime, playfully ask yourself, what is my Clair?

Training for Psychic Intuition

As I mentioned before, I work on a multidimensional level across disciplines, theories, and practices. Lately, as part of the explosion of this new world, the resurgence of ancient wisdom—paired with new science—has unleashed data-driven possibilities beyond measure.

I contend that all of us are multidimensional, and we just don't know it. We have access to messaging via our bodies and our higher senses. Composers like Mozart, inventors like Thomas Edison, mystics like Teresa Davila, and leaders like Gandhi and Martin Luther King, had their own particular communication with the unseen. There is a higher being, a higher purpose, a higher universe that wants to be in communication with us, and our human libraries are burgeoning with these stories in the form of clinical studies, mythologies, religious texts, and channeling, amongst many.

Okay, so how do we do this? How do we actually do this? How do we access this dialogue other than randomly? The boring answer is through self-study and practice. Even those who experienced their gifts spontaneously, found that they had to acquaint themselves with them and become unafraid in order to slowly, gently allow themselves a regular and structured conversation. Like anything else, practice produces expertise.

In the Appendix, I've put together an incredible toolkit with many different modalities to enhance your spiritual practice, support the cultivation of intuition, and foster a deeper connection to the divine, guiding you on your journey of self-discovery and spiritual growth. Experiment with different techniques to find what resonates most deeply with your own unique path and inner wisdom. Each of these modalities offers its own texture and ingredients for raising intuition and deepening connection to the divine. Exploring a combination of practices, tapping into your response to them, and seeking guidance from experienced practitioners and fellow walkers can help you discover the modalities that resonate most deeply with you.

These deeper connections can benefit anyone, but for Empaths, they are core to developing more fully into who you've always been meant to be.

Remember, this is *your* yellow brick road home.

Chapter 7
Build Your Bridge to Leadership

"As we let our light shine, we unconsciously give other people permission to do the same. As we are liberated from our own fear, our presence actually liberates others."

— Marianne Williamson

So where do we—the Empaths of this new era and especially those of us who are committed to healing—go from here? We use the tools we're practicing to create our own bridge to leadership.

If you've made it this far, you've already collected some of your most critical building supplies: self-knowledge, self-care, healing, understanding your gifts, and putting yourself in the equation. Voilá, you are nearing the crux of Empath Leadership.

Now we will set down another "brick" in your bridge to leadership. You don't have to look far at all to find it.

Claudia Cauterucci

A Long Look in the Mirror

Louise Hay, a pioneer in the self-healing movement, motivational author, and cancer and trauma survivor, was adamant about mirror work as an intensely direct modality for self-healing. Looking in the mirror and lovingly affirming yourself evaporates blankets of self-hate and inserts new self-love programming. Looking in the mirror, metaphorically, is also the Empath's road to recovery.

The Empath must put themselves back into the relational equation. In order to do so, they must look inside, acknowledge, and validate how gifted they are.

Entire systems are supplied by Empath abilities. In any corporation—meaning a group or body of individuals—the second-in-charge is often an Empath, working until all hours of the night, cleaning up the mess the narcissist left behind, harmonizing environments, finding the collaborative way to do things, and calling out the elephant in the room when there is an injustice.

When I watched the 2015 movie about Steve Jobs, Joanna Hoffman (played by Kate Winslet), his right-hand woman, embodied all the Empath characteristics, behaviors, woundedness, *and* sovereignty. She clearly sat in her throne—although could appear to others to be subjugated—because she boldly confronted him when no other would.

Recovery, self-study, and self-love moves Empaths into their prowess.

Empaths, the Bridge Starts with You

On so many occasions I have clients and workshop attendees ask me, do I have to keep doing these practices after I feel okay? The answer is a resounding YES. Do you have to keep brushing your teeth, moving your body, watering your plants, understanding your emotional reactions, making sure you have integration time, and realigning on a daily basis? *Hell yes.*

The bridge starts with you, baby. The bridge for you *is you*. The bridge for others IS YOU BRIDGING YOU. And well, yes, it's by maintaining our self-care and self-love practices. This is a non-negotiable in order to stay enthroned and well-docked in our root chakra. To do the work we are here to do—even and especially if that work is you being like Samson throwing down the temple pillars of ancestral trauma from both sides of your family with ferocity—this is a must.

You've done harder, my love.

Frame your day with self-love affirmations, meditation, mobility, kind words to your inner child, leaning into your back body, and music to automatically shift your energetic frequency. Why? Energy is the OG! Call it your RICHual and watch the abundance flow in. You've got this.

The next thing you know, you're more than a bridge. You're one hell of a lighthouse in a raging storm, standing tall, regal, and firm; shining the light; and securely attaching folks.

Claudia Cauterucci

Brick-by-Brick

The following are steps that include imaging, breathwork, and physical movements I recommend to Empaths. I cannot emphasize enough the importance of adjusting the body using these visuals. The Empath is ransacked by energies and compulsively leaves their body. Anchoring themselves in images and physical movements that embody the images is a package deal. The combination creates exponential shifts when Empaths are interfacing with their internal and external worlds. Note: When I say "you" here, I'm talking directly to Empath Leaders, but these practices can benefit anyone on a healing journey.

Ground Yourself

The root chakra power center is about belonging, safety, stability, survival, and attachment. If the root chakra is born into an environment where we are wounded, neglected, abused, and hurt, we begin to disconnect from the self and disassociate.

Visualize the root chakra below the pelvis, where we sit. The root chakra is the gateway to our grounding cord, where we feel connected or grounded to the earth. Picture that grounding cord as a tree trunk or pillar of light or a cord around us that leads us straight into connecting with the center of the Earth.

When we are disconnected and uncentered, feeling like we don't belong or like we're not okay because of the belief systems and because of the environment we were born into, we don't have any earth energy. We are ungrounded, not connected, and the root chakra contracts and disconnects from the grounding cord.

Visualizing the grounding cord has to be a daily meditative practice. Grounding the lower body and feeling its heaviness provides the sensation of secure attachment, belonging, and anchoring that was missing as a child.

The Empath has the energy of others: ancestral trauma from mom, dad, culture, race, etc. The body and the spirit cannot digest this much energy, so it lodges in the body and morphs into illnesses of undigested trauma. By breathing out those undigested pieces of trauma into the grounding cord, we can imagine the planet, Mama Earth (secure attachment image), absorbing it. I am reminded of the 12-step adage, "Let go and let God." Both depict the sensation of a loving parent taking our burdens and lightening our load.

The root chakra, grounded and clean, can heal and unfurl.

Empath Leaders: By grounding, we lay down the first chakra correctly; we rectify the home foundation. We lead in ancestral trauma healing, we lead in enthroning ourselves, and we lead in putting our face mask on first before helping others.

Calibrate Your Feelings

To relieve the oversaturated sacral chakra, drowning in energy, we must feel our feelings. The first stage of learning my Dynamic Meditation Method is centered on the sacral chakra. Saying yes to any and all feelings in order to help them leave the body is the first meditation: jealousy, envy, shame, betrayal, anger, and grief. We measure each feeling, we feel its texture, we allow its accompanying sensation, and we breathe it out, extending the breath on "yesssssssss." Like Rumi's poem, we welcome them all, like an honored guest, and—counterintuitively—we then clean out the body.

Once we know our feelings well, we are able to distinguish and identify them as separate from other people's feelings. We will not be lost in the feeling swirl. This is a re-parenting tool, lovingly listening to and allowing the feelings (energies) to exist and leave. We tell our inner child to share the truth about what they're feeling, validate the feelings, become experts on what we're feeling, and ultimately, know what we need.

Empath Leaders: This process actually increases our capacity to non-judgmentally let others have their feelings. We can better distinguish what's ours and what is theirs. In the Dynamic Meditation Method, inspired by Lester Levenson's work, I teach the "I am you and you are me" principle, which holds that the more we know our own feelings—our sense of betrayal, our shame, our racism, our rage, our lust, our desperate wanting—the dark, gooey corners inside of ourselves, then we can accept it and acknowledge them in others. When we accept ourselves, we are less likely to "other" people.

Lean Back into Your Body Throne

We move into the third chakra, the solar plexus, which is the seat of self empowerment. The solar plexus, which is right around the belly button, is the "I am." The solar plexus holds confidence, willpower, and masculine energy. Again, not related to gender, but it's out in the world in activating, making, doing, manifesting, presenting mode.

Before healing, instead of cording to the earth, we corded outside of ourselves with the front body, leaning forward. We found safety, security, sense of self, and groundedness in others instead of through our own grounding cord. It makes sense that the soul or our spirit moves higher and higher, into the upper body, into our thinking nature, which is why we become overthinkers as Empaths. We move into the head (masculine) in order to survive, abandoning our heart (feminine) and body.

We heal the solar plexus by releasing the energy that's no longer ours and by pulling back from energy that's leaking out of us. Essential here is noticing the use of our front body. Because we engage the world through our front body, it is easier to leave ourselves. We want to acknowledge and engage our back body by leaning back into the back body.

When we're in the front body, we are horizontally connected. We connect out. When we are in the back body, we are vertically connected and we reconnect to our body, our grounding cord, and to our Source. The backside of our energetic system, which connects and supports us—imagine the highway system that is your spine—is a straight connection to our higher self. When completely aligned, when seated in our throne with an upright posture, and when aware of our backside, our chakras light up like an airport landing strip, all the way up to our crown chakra, or our higher self.

We are relaxed, embodied, and enthroned.

Claudia Cauterucci

Empath Leaders: It's time to lean back. Embrace the regality of being centered and aligned to the self. Picture a lighthouse, with waves crashing about it, in the midst of storms, like the perfect one our world is in right now. With a strong lighthouse leader—or many—who get quiet, lean back, center, and hold the energies, the sense of a secure household will be gently re-established.

Radiate from Your Central Channel

When the root chakra is grounded and unfurled, the second and third chakras are in their place, and we are seated and embodied in our throne. **This positions us to radiate out.**

Our center channel is open, clean, and healed. From here, we can radiate our presence, our self-knowledge, our self-love. Imagine what we are doing with our children, our lovers, our workplace when that is our electromagnetic field! This is when we move into real empowerment.

The Institute of Heartmath says it best in their introduction: "Let's help activate the heart of humanity. It starts with each one of us. As you bring your physical, mental, and emotional systems into coherent alignment, you begin to experience increased access to your heart's intuitive guidance. Tuning into your heart's wisdom creates a profound shift within that helps you approach situations with more emotional balance, compassion, clarity, and personal confidence."

Empath Leaders: The Empath is entirely uncomfortable with showing off, but because of their care for others, can heed the call of showing up. Showing up with a clean presence, which

Build Your Bridge to Leadership

we can trust is not overly empathic or codependent, allows us to trust ourselves, and to trust the work we do for and with others. Our presence radiates healing and we are then living into our natural abilities as true light workers.

Protect Your Kind Heart with Your Posse

As the three musketeers said, "One for all and all for one." If you're a caregiver, a healer, someone who's shedding light on the world—and especially leaders, public figures, and CEOs—as Empaths you need your posse. In this case I mean posse in two ways: 1) your external posse of Empaths who are doing the same inner/outer work that you are; and, 2) your posse of boundary-setting tools—parameter, perimeter, and preference—which we will unpack later.

We've all gone through dark times in order to shed light for people. We are generous by nature and can't help but protect and provide for others in the world. We already know that if we have no parameters, no perimeter, and can't discern our preferences, we will leak! At ground zero or at your *a priori* self, if you will, you must protect the kind, generous heart with a parameter, a perimeter, and preference.

We also need others who are on the same path. As we are uplifters and way showers, we need places of wise rest. Yes, *wise* rest. We need others who aren't leaking, have claimed their central nervous system, and live in their prowess. We need others who see signs of the narcissist lurking when we are in the trenches. We won't do this alone anymore.

Empath Leaders: It is our innate gift to be light workers, way showers, and uplifters. Our urge is to show the world how to

Claudia Cauterucci

follow their most internal soul and to decree kindness, care, and empathy as a surviving and thriving tool for humanity. This is why our calling right now is so powerful. Unequivocal, loving self-protection comes first.

Use Your Pause-Power-Possibility-Prowess Life Kit

Why do you need a P-packed emergency kit? In case you forget everything else, in case you have little time before a board meeting, in case there is a shut down on the subway and the cabin goes dark, in case your child reveals something that freezes you, and in case you find yourself in the narcissistic haze, break the glass of the four p's emergency kit!

1. Take a **pause** (breathing helps).
2. Pausing provides the **power** to assess, discern, think, feel, or scan. Any martial arts movie or heroic endeavor highlights this in slow motion, because everything does slow down, i.e., the opposite of impulsive, compulsive leaning forward.
3. Power moves you into **possibility**. I declare that possibility is life's magic. What trauma most steals from us is the belief in possibility. A sign of healing is a resurgence of possibility. Possibility is life's orgasm wanting to express and create more life. Once we feel that things are possible ...
4. ... we can move into our **prowess**. Synonyms of prowess are accomplishment, aptitude, dexterity,

excellence, expertise, genius, mastery, and talent.

Yup. We pretty much want those.

But it all starts with the sacred pause.

Empath Leaders: The four p's life kit is easy to remember, it's simple, and IT'S EVERYTHING. Memorize it.

By restoring and coming home to themselves, the Empath will discover, discern, and decide, three primary pillars of leadership. But first you must know the dangers, and know them well. Like any Empath—but perhaps even more so because they have higher visibility—Empath Leaders must be vigilant about avoiding the dark, soul-sucking pull of the narcissist.

Chapter 8
Narcissists on the Prowl

"When we meet and fall into the gravitational pull of a narcissist, we are entering a significant life lesson that involves learning how to create boundaries, self-respect, and resilience. Through trial and error (and a lot of pain), our connection with narcissists teaches us the necessary lessons we need to become mature empaths."

— Mateo Sol

Right about now, you may be asking yourself, why should I learn about the narcissist? The narcissist is not only the prototype that most stalks and predates the Empath, the narcissist shows up in many forms in our human tapestry: the pedophile, the sex trafficker, cult leader, religious and political demagogue, scammer, tiger parent (from all cultures), the interminable victim, amongst others. Narcissism plagues our history, systems, and cultures, and supports structures like the untouchable wealthy, caste systems, slave labor, child labor, female invisibility ... basically all things oppression and domination.

The leadership aspect of this book requires that we understand narcissism as a leadership modus operandi; it permeates collective entities, such as corporations, cultures, and nations.

Individually, to have a PhD on ourselves, we must know what makes us sick, what's toxic to our system, and what we're allergic to, even when it tastes good.

Collectively, narcissism is the seed of all human wars and unless we understand it, we won't survive it.

The "Plug and Socket"

Discussing the enormous subject of the narcissist is a great undertaking. I cover the topic in only one chapter, which does not do it justice. There are prodigious speakers and authors, such as clinical psychologist Dr. Ramani Durvasula, Life Coach and co-dependency expert Lisa Romano, and expert coach in Narcissistic Abuse Recovery, Grace Being, who are doing great work in disseminating information about having a relationship with a narcissist and how to heal from it, and frankly, unapologetically debunking this age-old relational pattern from its pedestal.

It is essential to talk about the perfect "two-peas-in-a-pod, plug-and-socket" match between the narcissist and the wounded Empath. The narcissist gravitates towards the Empath's self-sacrificing and kind-hearted nature, and the wounded Empath finally feels seen and has the promise of being cared for. The narcissist sets camp inside the wounded Empath—who likely had a narcissistic caretaker—and digs a well which, over time, is more like an oil rig.

Here's why.

The narcissist struggles with an ever-constant intense and pervasive cauldron of feelings of shame, worthlessness, and self-loathing, which they can't acknowledge for fear of a free fall into the vast emptiness that is their internal life. It is because of this that the narcissist seeks out the gaze of others to bolster their view of themselves, which is extremely malleable and dependent. This constant seeking of feedback from others is a form of existential supply which is often called "narcissistic supply." Enter the Empath, which like the road to El Dorado, is a flowing source of supply in responsiveness, dedication, devotion, willingness, hard work, and empathy.

EMPATHS, BEWARE (flashing neon lights): It is important for the Empath to understand the disorder and the pathology of the narcissist because the wounded Empath is the socket to the narcissist's plug. The narcissist is attracted to the Empath because the Empath has so much supply, which falls on a spectrum of functionality, depending on their stages of healing:

- from genuine kindness to scared people-pleasing and fawning;
- from mature respect to self-deprecating reverence;
- from a willingness to not trump anyone to a profound instilled belief that they are inferior;
- from helpfulness that can dangerously turn into an all-consuming co-dependent over-availability.

Narcissists on the Prowl

From the narcissistic point of view, the range of healing is irrelevant because all of it is golden supply, and the demand is on! It is the Empath that must ultimately be the healed decision-maker of where their distribution goes on their road to sovereignty.

The narcissist docks into someone's well-intentioned and kind way of being as a way of filling themselves and hushing the self-hate whispers that torment them. The catch here is that none of this is reciprocal, and so the other person—this can be their own child, a partner, a parent, or a colleague—is often left depleted at best, and destroyed at worst. It is completely vampiric. I am reminded of the "Dementor" characters in the Harry Potter books, who fed off of human happiness and whose kiss literally sucked out a person's soul.

Narcissists have an extremely high level of dependence that is masked not only to themselves but to others because they tend to be the high-achiever in the room or the one with all the extras. Looks, fashion, vocabulary, adventures, material objects, hacks, know-hows, stories … the narcissist has it all! Picture Jeffrey Epstein and his web of offerings and connections. They seek others for their desperate need for admiration, self-escape, and undisclosed loneliness. Some men who are described as "players," who jump from sexual encounter to sexual encounter, claim to be independent and present as aloof, often experienced abandonment or neglect as children and thus have an acute fear of being alone. Their "playing" is a form of seeking narcissistic supply, mistaken for indifferent independence.

Narcissistic hypersensitivity to criticism drives them to be high-achieving, perfectionistic, and status-obsessed. They are always juggling where they fall on the societal ladder. Topping (and toppling) others is the only option to mitigate fears of incompetence, failure, worthlessness, inferiority, shame, humiliation, and losing control. Gaining social status and approval in order to avoid and combat these feelings will show up as exaggerating their skills, accomplishments, and name-dropping. They can quickly identify who the "most" or the "best" is in the room, whether by looks, title, or money, but mostly, by who can benefit them the most in terms of supply.

In many cases, the narcissist, like a heat-seeking missile, can spot the Empath in the room with ease because, many times, the Empath *IS* the best in the room. Generally, the Empath has an unacknowledged competence that was fortified for years for having to overcompensate in their families of origin. As a parentified child, the wounded Empath is the one who instinctively goes the extra mile and is "all-in" with their commitments because of their own desperate need to be seen and loved. This is not unlike the narcissist but from the other side of the coin. The narcissist plants their flag in the giving, over-pleasing Empath and like an electric car, finds a low-cost, endless source of free fuel. Sadly, this sometimes can be their own children.

The Driving Emotion Behind a Narcissist

The dominant emotion at the core of the narcissist is envy. It is a very primitive emotion and it is a form of early hatred. Being in touch with their emptiness and their inner lack is an excruciating experience, and everything outside of themselves is comparative, extreme, and dichotomous, either good or bad. For the narcissist, there are only two measures:

Am I superior or am I inferior? That is where they oscillate. The only choice is for others to be either idealized or devalued; otherwise, they are left with only themselves, which they experience as existential suicide. The narcissistic parent, for example, will compete with their own child, which is often why the Empath becomes so quiet about their successes and can't believe in them fully. The Empath fears the hostilities that may come their way.

Envy is a form of hatred and occurs because of a premature dethronement at an early childhood developmental stage. It could be that they were the first child and a second child was born close after, and hostile competition became a form of relating; or the critical abuse of a parent became an enemy from which to protect, combat, and emulate. The intense wounding—what is called the "narcissistic wound"—engenders a compulsive need to destroy all that's good, all that is beautiful, all that has any semblance of being superior. This envy is largely unconscious because it is too painful to consider. They are unaware of their envy, and when aware for a millisecond, it feels so excruciating that the impulsive and immediate defense is to devalue others, to have contempt, and to humiliate.

The paradox is that the Empath naturally succeeds. The Empath is innately hard working and gives their all because their human operating system is organically driven to harmonize environments. Whatever makes the environment better and more peaceful, not only to help others but to soothe themselves, they will do.

Like Cinderella, when Empaths know they can be the receptacle of hostile competition or narcissistic rage from a parent, a group, a boss, or a lover, they quickly learn to stay quiet about their gifts—to the point of not seeing them as such—and focus on just serving others and the environment. The narcissist comes after those gifts because they must have whatever it is that they envy. Unlike the Empath, they don't do so by learning, but rather by pillaging. Again, this is the vampiric narcissistic supply. Others are only a supply source. They will take or they will destroy.

This response happens with leaders all the time. It happens with bosses, and it's part of most political systems. If someone doesn't want to join their program or tow the party line, it automatically enfolds into the inferior/superior choreography. If someone gives them feedback that not all is good, they cope by blaming and projecting. Having contempt, devaluing, or discarding neutralizes the feeling of envy. It is a common war tactic to demean your enemy so that you can feel better about destroying them.

I'd like to add a bit of foreshadowing here. For centuries, the world has been dominated by a narcissistic paradigm of conquering and colonizing, which has had an impact on creating vastly unequal economic protocols and the inhumane treatment of other beings. This paradigm has infiltrated every corner of society, such as workspaces and business relations. The narcissist-Empath relational structure reappears later in the book as we discuss leadership paradigms.

The Lack of An Integrated Sense of Self

The narcissist is fragmented. The shadow self is completely amputated and disowned, and we see this in effect from the individual to the collective. This is what Carl Jung called the "collective unconscious." Studying the fragmented self is psychologically essential because so much of what we do in therapy has the aim of befriending all parts of ourselves, especially the parts we have disowned. Our amputations have a way of lurking, stalking, and ambushing us until we give them attention, healing, and love. After this alchemical welcome, they are quite transformed into psychological members we can integrate into our individuated SELF.

The narcissist cannot and will not do this. It is entirely unbearable. An example of collective fragmentation is not being able to fully accept and repair for the horrors of slavery. The repercussions of that dismemberment plague our society in each one of its corners; repair feels like a horrifying and unbearable long look in the mirror. Some experiences feel too terrifying to address, but we must—and we must do it in the companionship and witness of a loving other, like a therapist in a session or an Empath Leader for a community.

Narcissistic Relational Strategies

As Grace Being outlines in her book about narcissistic abuse recovery, *Let the Light Shine Through Your Deepest Wounds*, the narcissist lives as a manipulator. It is essential to understand their techniques and modus operandi to catch the red flags and respond effectively. Here are the predominant ones:

1. **Guilt-Tripping:** The narcissist induces guilt to make Empaths feel ashamed for standing up for themselves, so the Empath ends up apologizing and surrendering to the narcissist's desires. The Empath will generally self-reflect when accused

and often relegate themselves to the narcissist's version of the story.

2. **Lying:** To evade responsibility for their actions, the narcissist resorts to lying, aiming to control and persuade others. An insidious form of lying is "gaslighting," wherein the narcissist denies the Empath's version of the truth and directly lies about it being nonexistent, causing the reflective Empath to doubt themselves.

3. **Projection:** Blaming and shaming is a constant. The narcissist projects their own wrongdoings onto others, blaming someone else for their actions. No situation is ever due to them. This, by the way, is a solid red flag to spot early on. If, when telling their stories, everyone else is to blame…go ahead and moonwalk out, Empath.

4. **Love-Bombing:** This is an early-stage manipulative technique where the narcissist showers excessive attention, affection, or false promises (future-faking) to manipulate, get what they want, and keep an Empath beholden to them. Be forewarned, this stage is absolutely delicious, elusive, and dramatic. The Empath must heal before they date because their abandonment and neglect wounds are accomplices in the love-bombing.

5. **Changing Expectations:** Narcissists constantly shift expectations to keep others working hard to please them. Nothing is ever good enough, and more and more is required. Despite efforts, they rarely acknowledge or appreciate the efforts. Hoop jumping with no

reward is a short- and long-term strategy. Intermittent attention and fluctuations between hate and adoration create an addictive relational cycle. The secret to addictions is the intermittence of the high. The narcissist is the master of intermittence and the Empath can get in the weeds of trying to to understand why.

6. **Withdrawal/Silent Treatment:** Emotional manipulation involves punishment through affection and intimacy withdrawal and creates a power imbalance that leaves the Empath craving attention. The silent treatment is exceptionally cruel for the Empath because they felt invisible often as a child.

7. **Comparison:** Narcissists make their partners feel insecure by consistently comparing them to others and provoking feelings of unworthiness. This is the common "divide and conquer" strategy. A narcissistic parent does this to siblings; through comparing and criticizing each child, the parent creates a survival game wherein each child tries to gain the parent's approval by defeating the other sibling. These families lack trust and cannot seek comfort from each other in times of need. These families do not play because play requires safety. The wounding and scarring can last a lifetime unless the siblings are on board for communal healing.

8. **Triangulation:** This involves bringing in others to invalidate an Empath's feelings and reactions, aiming to validate the narcissist's point of view and sow uncertainty in the Empath. Threesomes are

the narcissist's happy place as it creates a distracting, competitive energy where the other two compete to serve the narcissist. Each contributes more and more supply—and submission—in order to "win" the narcissist's alliance.

Love Bombing to Just Plain Bombing

Once on the prowl, the narcissist will genuinely effuse their best behavior, their most intoxicating charm, their funniest jokes, and most well-read insights as the first strategic step in their ensnarement; this is commonly described as "love bombing" and is indeed, quite enthralling, especially for anyone who is in need of attention or affection in the first place, as often is the case of the wounded Empath.

Once past the love bombing stage, the narcissist has a difficult time regulating their emotions and will no longer hide —if not outright display—their sense of superiority via disdain, condescension, and verbal, emotional, and sometimes physical abuse. When they feel rejected or confronted, or when a boundary is placed upon their behavior, what typically ensues is a wrath of hateful or vengeful discourse, which is commonly referred to as *narcissistic rage* where they will incite a "smear campaign." An example of this is spreading rumors, public humiliation, financial and affection withdrawal, fear mongering, false accusations, and direct insults. Needless to say, divorcing a narcissist is a nightmare.

The language of the narcissist is to demean in order to feel superior. In a company, for example, a narcissistic boss or CEO might idealize the new kid on the block but then, very quickly be easily disappointed when expectations aren't matched, which is followed by discarding or devaluing. The Empath, if unhealed, will unknowingly collude with this devaluing because of their own low self-esteem and will rush to defend, explain, or concede.

The narcissist doesn't view people as separate from themselves. If you had a narcissistic mother or father, you are not a separate being: you are an extension of them. You are not seen as you are or at all. Having boundaries, separate opinions, vulnerabilities, or needs, is merely understood as a weakness to topple or dominate you. These are seen as opportunities to devalue you. If you were an Empath child, quickly putting yourself and your needs aside—invisibilizing yourself—was a survival mechanism. The narcissistic parent will compete with you because they need to feel superior to their children.

I call this "the swirl" or "the haze" because the Empath does not understand what is happening or why. They are in a perfect storm of confusion. As they are in a non-stop effort to please the narcissist, their psychic alarm system is blaring danger internally while they are barraged by narcissistic criticism externally. Nothing adds up, but they are not quite sure how because of " the haze." The Empath, and most humans, do not understand why the bully bullies and can not fathom their use of degradation and destruction in the face of feeling like they haven't done anything wrong.

Narcissism is a very severe personality disorder. Anyone under this shadow will doubt their own feelings, their own needs, their own perception, and their own intuition. What's important here is to note as an Empath is that these are the reasons that all this self-doubt, self-questioning, and not knowing how to follow your gut, begins to happen—even though, the whole time, you were the fixer, the solver, and the savior in the family, the relationship, or the job.

I address narcissistic personality disorder in this book because Empaths are raised, sought, and found by narcissists, and they are frequently paired with them, especially if unhealed. If you are an Empath, part of studying yourself requires studying the narcissist.

Narcissist-Empath Distinctions

Paradoxically, the Empath and the narcissist share a common origin story. They both generally have a traumatic past, characterized by abuse and/or neglect. They both have intense abandonment fears and their identity is erected on the gaze of others rather than a sense of self. The narcissist cannot bear to go inside because they fear a vast emptiness, while the Empath is barely aware that an inside exists because it's based primarily on serving others. Both run solo and have the "party-of-one" syndrome, but from opposite sides of the coin.

The primary and crucial distinction between them is that the Empath has a willingness to self-reflect. Like the narcissist, the wounded Empath has low self-worth and abandonment fears that contribute to self-degradation and negative acting out, possibly even demeaning another if at the height of their dysfunction, but they will ask themselves, *"Is this me? How am I contributing to this situation? Is this my fault?"* The narcissist will rarely, if ever, ask these questions. The way the Empath and the narcissist dramatically part ways from a similar past is in the choice of self-reflection.

Narcissism, Leadership, and Authority

The reason this is so important and central to this book from a leadership perspective is that there are all sorts of narcissists in the political, corporate, and entrepreneurial worlds.

One might venture to say that many thriving empires, governments, and political systems were erected on the narcissist/wounded Empath paradigm, wherein whole groups of people were deemed as inferior and yet were exploited for the "supply" they provided in the forms of labor, land, riches, and culture. This book serves to address this as an overarching concept and points the way to a rich discussion as to where we are headed as an emerging planet.

In work settings, the narcissist may invite feedback but upon receipt, will demean, scapegoat, or ignore the feedback. They will generally find a way to turn it back on the other person, family members, or team. Not only will they not take the feedback, they will go a step further and initiate a smear campaign. Once on the bad side of the narcissist, which is part of the relational trajectory, the attacks and accusations are interminable. A great example of this is legal responses to a woman being raped or sexually harassed and being called the instigator or the seductress. Women repeatedly, and until recently, opted for not confronting and not seeking help after these events. If not enveloped in waves of further public humiliation, they were enveloped in silent stonewalling for fear of the narcissist, in this case, either the corporate entourage or the legal system.

This isn't new. Since the beginning of time—since Cain and Abel, the story of one brother who killed another for his own gain—this dynamic has repeated itself. The history of the world has had example after example of the narcissistic paradigm being a dominant leadership model based entirely on hostile and fear-instilling maneuvers wherein the endgame is total and complete dominance. Our history books are rife with these stories, and they are still happening today.

This book is an invitation to become experts in spotting this leadership archetype and is proposing its exact counterpart. As one of my co-authors, Charles Martinez describes it: "This book puts forward the upside-down kingdom where the Empath feels empowered and skilled, is no longer serving the master, and has conviction about a collaborative world which reflects their values."

A brief but strong reminder here: Once Empaths stop serving the master, the narcissistic system collapses because the fuel source—the Empath's profound insecurity and desire for belonging—is unavailable. Self-governance and sovereignty are the name of the game.

Chapter 9
A Paradigm Shift

"A person needs new experiences. They jar something deep inside allowing him to grow. Without change, something sleeps inside us, and seldom awakens. The sleeper must awaken."

— Dune (1984 version)

Now that we know more about the Empath's inner world, and we start moving into the leadership aspect of their nature, let's explore their outer world, which is the world most of us were dropped into. Let's start by elevating the drone to a bird's eye view of our world from a particular paradigm: the lack matrix. But first, a few words about paradigms and why and how we have the power to change them.

Claudia Cauterucci

From Perceptual Fields to Beliefs to Paradigms

Let's understand the perceptual field, a term originating from Gestalt psychology and used as a psychological organizational construct. It basically means (baby-talk here) that we take in information through our senses, and because our perceptual field includes so many stimuli flying at us, like bugs on a windshield, it is impossible for our brains to process and make sense of it all unless we siphon it through a filter that fits what we already know.

Two people can look at the same image and have vastly different interpretations of it. The image a person sees depends on what they perceive as background or foreground. I give the example of depressed clients who, when watching a rom-com, may only remember the break-up scene or the rainy day. The anxious client will remember the awkward moments or the cliffhangers as excruciating. The overall gist will have the overlay of their perceptual field, not only because it's the most practiced version of life but because it's genuinely hard to take in all that is coming at them. Relaxed love or easy laughter often feels outside of their perceptual field, hence the depressive and anxious responses.

The danger with perceptual fields is that if repeated with enough consistency, they become beliefs. Beliefs become our reality, the paradigms through which we engage the world. On the other hand, the embedded gift in perceptual fields is that we can learn to consciously choose new ones. Depending upon where we shift and hold our gaze, we can then create a new reality.

A Paradigm Shift

Enter the hero of paradigm reprogramming: neuroplasticity! Neuroplasticity provides us with the "yes we can" scientific hope that change through choice is possible. As Wikipedia defines, "Neuroplasticity...is the ability of neural networks in the brain to change through growth and reorganization. It is when the brain is rewired to function in some way that differs from how it previously functioned."

What excites me about neuroplasticity is that it has promised us this truth: our brain can heal, continue to grow, and create new neural nets, no matter what we've been through! We can expand beyond our traumatic backdrop and transform the color of our lenses to well-adjusted, trauma rising, rose-colored ones.

What's the key to neuroplasticity? Having or creating a new experience. New experiences include all the healing modalities to which we have access OR your relationship with a caring adult (lover, mentor, therapist, trainer, colleague) OR traveling to other countries OR communion with the divine OR 12-steps OR meditation, and oh, so many more ORs. Neuroplasticity promises us a future through an experienced, reformed, and chosen personal vision. As I tell my clients, it's not that the trauma goes away, it's that through a new perceptual field via a healing experience, we can dim the lights on it and spotlight somewhere else.

Sigh. Don't get me started on my love affair with neuroplasticity.

Paradigms are a form of perceptual field in that they amass a combination of perceptual fields into one model. When we adhere to a paradigm, we are adhering to an understanding of our world. The world is a combination of multiple paradigms; some are larger and stronger than others. We are dropped into this world into a group of people with several established paradigms. Our family, culture, race, socioeconomic class, and religion are paradigms. They are a merengue of psychological programming, belief systems, emotions, sensations, and set of rules that form it. Other terms we can use to describe paradigms are neuro-associations, schemas, and patterns, all based on a set of hardwired neural networks.

As children, we're given the paradigms we are dropped into and swallow them whole. Remember the word introject? This psychological word describes when we accept a concept without looking at it, digesting, or discerning about it. As children, we couldn't make any of those calls; children imitate without question. Children trust. Adults can question.

The Sleeping Volcano

The catch here is that most adults don't question because they are unaware. The psychoanalytic premise that most of our existence is plopped on a glacier of mired, entangled experiences and memories that we unknowingly hide from our conscious life is true for most humans. This undiscovered glacier is known as "the unconscious." When I teach, I call it the sleeping volcano. The sleeping volcano looks beautiful when undisturbed, but when triggered, explosions happen, lava burns its paths, and it leaves behind a trail of destruction, like when you wake up next to someone you don't know and can't remember how you got there. Spoiler alert: It can also awaken us to our need for strategic self-knowledge and self-mastery.

A Paradigm Shift

Bear with me here. I *promise* it's going to be worth it.

This glacier or sleeping volcano is an accumulation of reactions to life that are based on survival responses. Picture several masses of unwanted survival knots inside of this volcano, formed by our introjects. Like mean flying monkeys, they unexpectedly show up to terrorize us as high-drama, emotional moments that are trying to get our attention. The invitation is to become conscious of the message of these emotional "call-outs" in order to uplevel.

More often than not, our common story is that we are born into this earth, into a well-trodden story woven by others—our parents, our school, our religion, our cults—who, like on a factory line, passed us down the unwanted knots of survival reactions, that now form a sleeping volcano. Lo and behold, while sitting on this personal sleeping volcano, we are receiving dictation from our inherited paradigms in surround sound. The "red pill" was not yet available to catapult us out of unconscious living.

The Blue Pill World

In the 1999 classic film, *The Matrix*, there is a scene where the main protagonist, Neo, is at an existential crossroads and is offered a red pill or a blue pill. The pills are symbolic of the choice before him. The red pill means a willingness to learn a potentially irreversible, life-changing truth, and the blue pill means to remain in an unconscious, contented or suffering ignorance. This book is my version of the red pill where we strap on our gear, get our water bottles, form a caravan—with wise sherpas, of course—and explore the volcano while it's sleeping.

Claudia Cauterucci

Amanda Flaker, the new world pioneer and philosopher we mentioned earlier, exploded overnight with over 40,000 YouTube followers during the pandemic with her description of the current state of our world within what she defines as the "lack matrix paradigm." It goes something like this:

The world we were dropped into is a paradigm that is fueled by a gnawing, chasing sense of lack. The foundational belief is that we are not enough and that there isn't enough. I repeat: All humans are not enough and there isn't enough. And so what logically ensues is a race to prove who is worthy of receiving the little that is available. In some circles, this is translated into humans being born "sinners," lower caste, dark-skinned, the weaker gender, last in line....you get it. We are born "not enough" to be worthy. Our human programming—mine, yours, theirs—is congealed in lack.

If we are not enough and there is not enough, we have to fight for what is there. How do we fight for it? We have to prove ourselves worthy. We have to compete for the resources, any resources: mom's love, dad's attention, SAT rankings, credit scores, dress sizes, penis sizes, square footage, sibling placement. We must jump through eternal, never-ending hoops of worthiness.

Add extra trampoline work to avoid the booby traps, the mudslides, the quicksand, and the straight-up bullet-dodging—depending on race, ethnicity, gender, sexuality, and economic class—to compete for worthiness. Worthiness asks, *"Will you love me? Am I deserving of care? Do I have the right to love, happiness, work, education, and evolution?"*

A Paradigm Shift

Evolution, which means, growth into better. We even wonder whether we have the right to grow.

When there is not enough, we hustle, compete to survive, elbow out, and pounce on the last slice of pizza. The lack matrix forces and establishes a paradigm of war within ourselves, with others, and with the planet. It is *The Hunger Games* as we race against other humans to beat them and win, proving that we are worthy. The options are easy: We are either winning or losing, good or bad, rich or everyone else. From the school cafeteria to the dating apps, from college admissions to Nordstrom's dressing room, from where we sit on a bus to whom we're allowed to kiss, from who has permission to talk to God and who declares themselves as God, from Abel and Cain fighting for their father's approval ... it's a legit, non-stop worthiness war.

Within the backdrop of war, the main characters of the lack matrix are the victim, the savior, and the aggressor. They each need each other in order to exist. Without an aggressor, there can be no victim, and there can be no savior. The trick here is that how the victim, savior, or aggressor manifests is mostly a game of musical chairs.

On the planetary landscape, we can see cases where the victim of human rights transgressions later becomes the perpetrator of those same aggressions, and other nations are rallying, discussing, and negotiating whose role is to be the savior. In my studies of the Cold War, for example, it was clear that, at the time, the U.S. saw itself as saving the Central American nations from the aggressive rule of impending communism. In retrospect, and for many Central Americans, the American presence during that

Claudia Cauterucci

time felt like an alliance with narcissistic leaders who were not safeguarding their people's interest. The point here is that whether that presence was in service or not, whether it saved or not, doesn't compare to the fickleness of the unconscious human story in which one day we hate the aggressor, then we become the violent aggressor if triggered, and we ultimately crucify the savior for interfering with the status quo.

I know this was true in my times of deep unconscious trauma, and it's true for families with an alcoholic or abusive parent. Our vow to never be like them, if left unprocessed and radically unhealed, will show up in multiple configurations. Our allegiance to the codependent parent, who may have "saved" us from the abuse on occasion, may later become rage that they never left the abuser. The savior becomes the victim, the victim the aggressor … and so on. And thus, this is the human game of musical chairs between victim/savior/aggressor.

What if, through deep healing, self-study, and self-mastery (which is now at our literal fingertips), we become self-governing? What if we learn that we can steer our own ship? What if we identify our needs, wants, and preferences and raise a generation who can do more of the same? What if we have Empath Leaders bringing victims, saviors, and aggressors to a communal table for discussion of this paradigm? *This* is the call and the promise of the world that Empaths can help us realize.

Back to our existing reality. In the lack matrix, who determines who is worthy, and how do we determine worthiness? It looks something like this:

A Paradigm Shift

- If you're born into money, you're worthy.
- If you have a certain shape, you're worthy.
- If you're a certain color, you are worthy.
- If you're in a certain level of education, you are worthy.
- If you're a certain religion, you are worthy.
- If you're a boy, you are worthy.
- If you're married and have children, you are worthy.
- If you're heterosexual, you are worthy.
- If you are "good," you are worthy.

The history of humanity, politics, social standings, social media, inner dialogue is all engulfed, dripping in the lack matrix.

Who is doing this? Humans! You and me. Humans are putting other humans smack in the middle of the Colosseum, raising our thumbs up or down, and clapping for on-the-spot physical and psychological executions according to group agreements on worthiness. Are you enough, yay or nay? It's no wonder the Korean movie *Squid Games* became a global blockbuster: Humanity saw itself. Killing each other due to lack has been the undercurrent fueling our human societies for as far back as we have recorded it. It's also no wonder that I'm associating so many movies to the lack matrix, because watching the darkness of lack matrix unfold is what we are most addicted to watching.

As we are taught to play this unconscious game of human Jenga, we actually leak out our birth-given worthiness, in our attempt to prove ourselves. I call this "the leaky boat syndrome." When born into the lack matrix, the root chakra has cracks and leaks all over the place. Our leaky boat is when we see ourselves as less than, always struggling, underprivileged, ashamed, guilty, and embarrassed (a huge leak). When we don't feel like we belong and are feeling left out of that group or the other group that seem to have the code of worthiness, we are leaking our worthiness in torrents. Our whole human system is based on hoop jumping, and it all leads to one place and that place is that we are not worthy of love. We are bad.

Shame, shame, shame, shame, shame. Like the residual gunk inside the oven that feels impossible to remove—like the food crumbs turned into paste between the crevasses of the car seats—we shame and blame, shame and blame, layering the lack matrix lasagna. And humanity runs on this fuel.

Lester Levinson wisely said, "When the love is complete, the problem is solved." From 23 years of private practice, 50,000 hours of individual and group sessions, and 200+ self-healing workshops, I have discovered this over and over: At the very bottom layer of our woundedness is that we believe that we are unlovable because we are bad. This belief provides a strange, predictable comfort that the bullying, shaming, and competing lack matrix world does not.

At least feeling bad resembles an answer to the question that puzzles us as humans, the one we just don't get, the last crossword puzzle sequence: Why do humans treat other humans this way?

The War Vibe

The central, and for me, most powerful, tenet of Amanda's lack matrix model is the insidious, seeping, equal oppor-

A Paradigm Shift

tunist nature of what she coins "the war vibe." It is rampant, penetrating, and long-standing—and it takes no prisoners. The irony is that it's also inherently promiscuous, getting into bed with whoever is on top or choosing sides depending upon what's trending. It's also subtle and sneaky, disguising itself as "doing good" or "being the good ones" even when using the exact war tactics it's fighting. Easy examples were the religious crusades, where they were killing for "the glory of God," or when one nation colonized another after having won the fight for its own freedom. It's the kicking-the-dog syndrome when having been harassed at work.

A special note here: Amanda, a high level, conscious Empath herself, has been able to "see," outline, and track these human incongruences and double standards. Not being able to bear the elephant in the room, she's calling the war vibe out! She trumpets the call to love our humanity by first witnessing the absurdity of our repetitive pendulum swings of "us versus them." Amanda, a natural Empath Leader, is an exact embodiment of where this book is headed. Behold, an enthroned Empath using her prowess. It is no wonder that she became a YouTube sensation during the pandemic. Humans, especially Empaths, needed and heeded her call.

Feudalism, slavery, the Inquisition, apartheid, the caste system, and the Holocaust, have all started and ended in the same place: the hatred of humanity. Humans are paying a very high price to participate in a game that only requires another bribe of worthiness at the next rung. That price is our proximity to extinction.

Aren't you just exhausted from reading this? The lack matrix paradigm runs us ragged and, historically speaking, has no end in sight.

Claudia Cauterucci

When we are born into a landscape that has lack as its core and is fueled by the belief that only certain people are worthy, a war is constantly brewing. Humanity's daily existence requires a fight to satisfy the worthiness craving and to get some relief. We wake up asking, "Who's on top now?"

Fret not. This paradigm, a fermented melange of childhood wounds and environmental messaging that makes us believe that we are unworthy of love, is merely one program running, albeit a monstrous one. What's the anomalous hack? You're reading it. It's the blue pill of consciousness. It's your brain's brilliant capacity for change. It's the terrifying choice to say, I AM WORTHY.

Bam! We are catapulted out of lack! **That goes for you, human, and for you, Empath.**

The Triple D's

You get to *discover, discern, and decide* what you believe. Take inventory. Do you want to believe in the messages from your culture, your childhood, your group, your religion, your race, your ethnicity, your ranking, your history? Either way is perfectly fine as long as you are the conscious chooser and the decider. Like a buffet, you get to pick and choose which parts of the story you were born into you want, but not without deep trauma work first. Because trauma is not just the Empath's story; it's humanity's story.

Discovery, discernment, and deciding are not for the faint of heart. In *The Matrix*, a grand moment is when Neo jumps from a window, and lands heroically; it is pretty frightening to behold. It's the same with the lives of most innovators,

A Paradigm Shift

creative outliers, and daring pioneers: They seem dangerous as well as beautiful to behold ... in retrospect. In the moment, their decisions can feel scary and lonely. But thanks to them, we can shift our gaze and access new paradigms.

Lastly, know that sovereignty triggers the punishment/reward firewalls, and the inner loudspeaker will repeatedly remind you that unless you dress a certain way, look a certain way, act a certain way, tap dance, and jump high, you are not worthy. Lack is the belief in conditional love based on walking in lockstep, and it's a program that has enslaved us all out of uniqueness and diversity. Humanity has not been able to escape it, but remember that whole "knowledge is power" thing?

The truth will set us free, and the truth is you matter, your feelings matter, and your contribution to the human equation matters. And I would venture to say that *your contribution matters now more than ever.* When we abandon our truth and ourselves in order to stay in the lack matrix—chasing the carrot of being deemed worthy by someone else—we vote for the us-versus-them war vibe.

Empath, please hear me here: When you bypass your truth, your needs, and your feelings to make everyone else happy, you abandon your true leadership gifts. Empaths are natural harmonizers and are unconsciously choosing to pay the price by falling on their own sword to maintain harmony.

The time has come for you to fully take hold of your gifts as committed and empathic cooperators, collaborators, peacekeepers, and harmonizers for this swirling world that verges on its own self-destruction.

Claudia Cauterucci

To Lead, the Empath Must First Break This Vow

In order to lead, the Empath must be free and out of the lack matrix. This book has a decree: *The Empath must stop suffering for the world but rather lead with sovereign, well-earned joy.*

The Empath understands humanity's pain. The Empath, and the human, goes to sleep to their own experiences because they hurt. Traumatic childhoods and ancestral trauma hurt. Humans keep playing out the pattern of pain because they are not free; self-medicating and sleepwalking are the name of the human game in order to shut out pain and lack. The side effect is that we shut down our most amazing human operating system: our feelings. By staying unconscious and numbing ourselves out, the sneaky narcissist pounces, and the next thing humanity knows, we are taking a right onto the exit that reads, "Road to Extinction."

Empaths are holding so much for the human network. Empaths feel on some unconscious level that they have to hold the world. The unconscious vow is that the Empath must suffer until the world is not suffering. The Empath will codependently do the feeling work for the world and will not let others feel. Empaths are the interceder for humanity because they feel. So they must lead by example and by rising above trauma.

When the Empath is holding too much, or if they shut down, they are colluding with extinction. Not feeling is choosing to no longer be human. If the Empath is holding too much suffering for the world, they disintegrate. What's

A Paradigm Shift

happening right now is that the Empath is waking up all over the planet and asserting their will. Through books like this, programs, podcasts, and fiery awareness, the Empath is connecting to their desires, preferences, and life force.

The moment for conscious leadership is now.

Chapter 10
The Heart of Leadership

"Dare to connect with your heart. You will be lifting not only yourself and those you love and care about, but also the world in which you live."

— Doc Childre, HeartMath Founder

Kind, but Not Stupid

By now, my hope is that you have a deeper understanding of the true meaning of Empaths—and more importantly, a deeper understanding of the power they hold to change the world. As we push forward to the role of the Empath Leader, let's look at where these two concepts—Empaths and Leadership—connect.

The heart of this book—and the connection between these concepts—is big, beautiful, pulsating, and fierce. It is alive with power.

The Heart of Leadership

It is the kind heart of the Empath.

We look for and value a kind heart in others. Is the flight attendant kind, not just doing her job? Is the Uber driver kind, not just doing his job? Is the doctor kind, takes their time, not just doing his/her job? My premise is that kindness initiates care. Care helps us survive together. A movement begins with many. Many who care will save humanity and the planet.

Kindness is what helps people help others escape from oppressive governments. Kindness offers water when we're thirsty. Kindness comes and visits—it doesn't just send texts, but visits—when we're sick. Kindness offers a seat in a crowded subway. Kindness hosted Anne Frank in an attic and powered the underground railroad. Children treating animals with kindness is an actual diagnostic assessment.

Kindness is seen as a soft skill, but it's truly the courageous heart of this planet because it is the great connector of our human operating system. It allows for seeing the humanity in another human; it allows for seeing ourselves in them.

Here's the trouble: In our human history, having a kind heart is how we have been wounded and traumatized. In the narcissist/Empath dynamic, kindness has been the entryway into abuse and subjugation. Images of Native Americans rowing their canoes, laden with fruits, flowers, and gifts, to welcome foreigners sailing close to their shores, come to mind.

Here lies the confusion: Being overly empathic, without boundaries or discernment, without emotional regulation, is the issue—not kindness. Extracting oneself from the relational equation without self-love or self-governance, is the issue—not kindness. Abandoning holistic alignment—wherein thoughtfulness, gut feelings, and spiritual guidance are acknowledged and heeded is the issue, not kindness. Being deprived of knowledge, blinded by the veil of lack, and mob mentality, are the issue—not kindness.

The kind heart is central to our humanity. As Victor Frankl, centuries of Buddhist philosophy, and the chorus to Jesus' message announce, caring-kindness is the coup d'état that propels humanity not only away from extinction but also to its next level of evolution.

We must then fully study, embody, and understand the kind heart and not have it randomly, spastically, or impulsively be the saboteur of our psychological prowess.

Parameter, Perimeter, and Preference

The heart is the place from which we Empaths radiate our electromagnetic field, our gifts, our prowess, and our genius. The Empath must commit to staying open because it is with the heart that we care, and care is the code to creating exponential prosperity and success.

Empath's sensitivity and associations to words that have been loaded for millennia with misaligned meaning to the kind heart have challenged ways that the Empath can easily digest this new leadership paradigm. "Protecting the heart" can put them in hyper-vigilant code yellow or orange, scanning interactions for danger. "Boundaries around the heart" can feel like we are closing it off, barricading it, or building a fortress around it. I'm here to tell you that Empaths *can* live
r heart and commit to it while also sagely
it.

The Heart of Leadership

Like Amanda's phrase, "keeping ourselves in the equation," these words are generally used in a mathematical context: parameter and perimeter. We'll use them in service of redacting our own contract around our committed heart.

A parameter is defined as a limit that affects how something can be done. As we study ourselves and self-heal, we generate the parameters we need around our heart. For example, you may decide that unless someone is on the path of self-growth or of healing ancestral trauma and behaviors, they are not the best partner for you. Because we are hard-wired to absorb energies and harmonize our environments, who the Empath chooses to live with is non-negotiable. They must be doing the work of recovery or healing.

Good questions for a parameter are:

1. With whom and how do they want to wake up and go to sleep?
2. Are they moody?
3. Are they generous with their time, attention, and finances?
4. Are they helpful?
5. Are they sweet?
6. Do they initiate care and affection?
7. Are they an Empath, and where do they fall on the spectrum?
8. Are they committed, without co-dependent pushing or pulling, to their inner work?

The other word is perimeter which is defined as the outline of a physical area. Our heart has a perimeter—not barricades, not a fence, not barbed wire, and not doors without locks either. Nobody can come in and emotionally invade, molest, and pillage. Picture a heart with a bold line outlining it and carefully colored inside the lines; it does not bleed or obstruct emotions. It just defines where their sovereign self ends and the other person begins. The perimeter provides a sacred pause for discerning passageways, in quantity and quality.

Good questions for perimeter are:

1. Do I feel a haze?
2. Does something feel off or creepy?
3. Was that a jab?
4. Do I want to help or save?
5. Do I get a sense that I am reading between the lines?
6. Do I feel a silent hypervigilance?
7. Do I feel like I'm rushed to please?
8. Do I feel like if I don't, they will be mad or punishing?
9. Does this story, image, song, or movie feel like an emotional molestation (creating a feeling I don't want but to which I feel obligated or forced to endure)?

Empaths struggle with the idea of boundaries for a few reasons. Their boundaries as children were not respected. Empaths didn't know about energetic and psychic boundaries, and so it always felt natural to be in a haze of energetic confusion, where knowing where they begin and others end was never defined. Empaths also receive identity rewards for being "boundaryless" and serving as a constant source of supply. Boundaries, then, become a way of feeling bad about themselves because, if unhealed, they don't know who

The Heart of Leadership

they are if they mark boundaries. Boundaries trigger abandonment fears. Lastly, the sensitive and kind-hearted Empath feels that if they set a boundary, they are hurting someone else's feelings.

This is where preferences work beautifully. Preference is defined as "a greater liking for one alternative over another or others." It's so much gentler than a boundary and yet marks it. It embeds non-judgement of the other or the self, because it is merely a preference. And for you, healing, self-exploring, discerning, and deciding Empath, your preferences are well researched. You get to prefer and not hurt feelings; you get to prefer your parameter and perimeter; you get to prefer and pivot out of anything that feels like emotional molestation. Preference protects because it creates an energetic circle that doesn't attack others while delineating an invite-only stance.

Some good questions for preference are:

1. Is it mutual?
2. Is it balanced?
3. Is it reciprocal?
4. Do I get in the way that I give?
5. Do I like this?
6. Do I regret it after?
7. Do I wonder why I keep doing something?
8. Are they kind to me?
9. Am I depleted or energized?
10. Are they thinking of me?
11. Do they notice me?
12. Do I feel respect or fear?

Claudia Cauterucci

Do you see that there is a choice to kindness? By having a parameter, a perimeter, and a preference, we can commit to the kind heart.

Empath Leader, you *must* know that kindness is your strength, your belief, your commitment, and your conviction. It adds to your prowess.

The fiery, kind heart is your crest.

Strong kindness is your superpower—and it's the power that ushers in the new way for this new world and new era.

Chapter 11
Leadership and The Rise of The Meek

"Leadership is not about being in charge. Leadership is about taking care of those in your charge."

— Simon Sinek

Blessed Be the Meek

But are Empaths truly meek or merely the powerhouses that are not showing up?

What the pandemic showed us—with real data—is that people are looking for leaders, guides, coaches, therapists, and advisors, who can help them find meaning and purpose in this new planetary landscape. A study done by McKinsey & Company in December of 2020, reported that the pandemic served as a before and after measure for highlighting corporations that validated their employees' work-life upheaval, with 50 percent rating empathy as the top factor. In their segment, "Leadership in Crisis: Responding to the coronavirus outbreak and future challenges" notable mentions were a leader's capacity to respond with calmness, empathy, decisively, and with equanimity. They remind, "It is vital that leaders not only demonstrate empathy but open themselves to empathy from others and remain attentive to their own well-being."[1] It's as if they were foreshadowing this book.

British management and sustainability legend John Elkington coined the term the triple bottom line or TBL: a management philosophy that equally prioritizes financial growth, individual well-being, and planetary health, better known as the PPP, profit, people, and the planet.[2] Putting humans first is not only the conversation that's trending on LinkedIn and in board rooms these days, it's what the planet is requiring following the pandemic's upheaval. Harvard Business School professor Rebecca Henderson says, "It's possible to do the right thing and make money at the same time." Whether you call it TBL, PPP, or win-for-all, it's the Empath Leader's life calling.

But it doesn't stop there.

Will Prebel, brand expert and AI specialist, in his LinkedIn article on emerging media and tech, describes that Empath Leaders bring something incredibly powerful to the table. "The primary power of an Empathic Leader is vision. Empathic leaders can easily see many sides of a situation because their intuitive understanding is so holistic. When placed into an environment, an Empath can absorb all of it, learning and adapting much faster than the average person." He claims that it is the Empath who can guide corporations through digital transformations, help cities build inclusive communities, and nurture startups that create more opportunities for everyone.

Leadership and The Rise of The Meek

Empaths will be the healers who *bridge* the gap between practices like yoga, meditation, grounding, the "clairs," and energy medicine with the traditional healthcare system. As technology continues to shape our world and the fear of job loss as AI proliferates, leaders who can self-regulate, think critically, empathize deeply, hold space for difference, and inspire others to do the same, are in high demand. Not to mention those who teach resilience in a changing world. Resilience in the face of adversity, who you gonna call? Not Ghostbusters, but Empath Leaders.

I hope you now see that being an Empath or empathic does not mean being soft or weak; nothing could be further from the truth. The traditional leadership paradigm with the relentless pursuit of power for power's sake is slowly dismantling.[3] As we evolve, we're realizing that true strength lies in vulnerability and connection. That's the kind of impact Empath Leaders can have. Is it any wonder that Brené Brown's research on vulnerability has made her a top advisor to the most prominent CEOs nationally and internationally? Her TedTalk, "The Power of Vulnerability," has millions of views. For a soft skill, it sure is hitting hard!

Ultimately, I see the Empath Leader as not just a label for a select few but as a blueprint for the kind of leaders we need in the future. Heck, for now! It's go-time.

Ironically, the Empath is leaking their sovereignty by not embodying themselves fully. Once sitting on the throne of their root chakra, with a calm central nervous system, in tune with their prowess, with their creative juices pumping and their will at the helm, the Empath is unstoppable. Not only are their organic inclinations available, but their wounds are now their gifts.

Humanity, the planet, and the times are crying out for a new type of leader who can respond to a turbulent environment using intuition, self-reflection, compassion, and emotional intelligence. By nurturing these qualities in ourselves and future generations, we're not just reducing suffering—we're paving the way for a future filled with abundance for all.

Your Wounds Are Your Gifts

In the 1990s, psychologists Richard Tedeschi and Lawrence Calhoun coined the term post-traumatic growth or PTG. Their theory posits that trauma can have great transformational value. The central idea is that people who have endured and worked through psychological struggle after trauma can find a light at the end of the tunnel and can ultimately grow from it. I call this the high alchemy of "trauma rising."

Self-report assessments inventory positive responses to five specific areas to determine the individual's transformational measurements:

- Appreciation of life
- Relationships with others
- New possibilities in life
- Personal strength
- Spiritual change

Dr. Julie Lopez—psychologist, trauma expert, speaker, dear friend, and author of the book, *Live Empowered: Rewire*

Leadership and The Rise of The Meek

Your Brain's Implicit Memory to Thrive in Business, Love, and Life—says it beautifully about her own trauma as an adoptee:

> "In fact my own struggles following relinquishment trauma and ongoing attachment struggles, have led to some of the biggest strengths I possess as a healer: perception, deep respect, compassion and 'the eye for potential.' I have found that every single one of my thousands of clients, spanning 30 years of clinical practice, who have faced adversity have experienced with it, post-traumatic growth."

Is this an echo of everything you've read so far? I hope so because we're about to PTG this whole thing.

The Empath Leader Resume: The C-Suite

I titled this the Empath C-Suite—playfully because it's all "c" words—but truly because it embodies what the Empath provides in any relationship, group, team, or leadership position. The C-Suite also serves as a helpful relational model that the Empath can require in choosing their own relationships, team, or leadership structure.

The C-Suite is a combination of the Empath's natural leanings as well as the transmutative effect of transforming their wounds into gifts.

If you are choosing the path of the Empath Leader, these Cs serve as both a celebration of your gifts, and as a reminder.

Commitment: You are inherently committed and devoted; you have an "all-in" way of working, loving, and living. You've learned to search for where you belong and so you understand and provide belonging to others. *As a leader, you will stay late and go the extra mile because of your passionate commitment.*

Care: Care is attached to and separate from love. You inherently recognize where care is needed and provide it. *As a leader, your attention to others and to detail will distinguish you from many. You will deeply care about whether a corporation, a family, or humanity thrives.*

Competence: You are highly competent because you love to study and deep dive. It comes naturally because you've been such a hard worker. Competence turns the Empath on! *As a leader, competent excellence is natural because you've had to earn your stripes multiple times. Hoop jumping does not intimidate you, and when healed, neither does excelling.*

Curiosity: You are extremely curious because you love to learn and grow. Curiosity enables both. You also need to be stimulated (note to self when choosing a life partner). *As a leader, you will ask good questions, you will be thorough in your research, and you will be able to see multiple points of view because you are curious about them.*

Cooperation and Collaboration: You work, love, and live best from a cooperative and collaborative approach. Teamwork is your jam because you feel energized and vibrant to move in growth with others. You know the ineffective pain of subjugation. *As a leader, you value a cooperative and collaborative approach because you value everyone's internal harmony, and workplace harmony, see genius, and respect imperfections.*

Connection: You need to have deep connection because it allows for trust. *As a leader, you are adept at relationship building.*

Comprehension: You truly want to understand how someone else is feeling and why they are in or out of alignment. *As a leader, you will strive to resolve conflict through active listening, understanding someone's world, and adjusting. Leaders must comprehend others in order to be strategically sound.*

Convening: You easily get along with many types of people and tend to bring them together. You follow "the bridge archetype." *As a leader, you will be able to lead many types of people from diverse backgrounds and bring them together in spite of the stress created by differences.*

Communion: You want to truly be with people and feel present. It's about breaking bread and conversing together without distractions. *As a leader, your urge for communion will provide a set and setting based on communal care, presence, and fun. Communion ensures longevity and stability in work settings.*

Compassion: You deeply feel what others feel. In Spanish, "compassion" literally means "with passion." *As a leader, you will lead with compassionate passion, both offering trust and safety.*

Composure: You, as an enthroned Empath, have composure. You know to self-regulate in spite of your triggers. *As a leader, calm composure is essential in adversarial situations, conflict resolution, and strategic planning. People feel safe with a leader who keeps their composure.*

Claudia Cauterucci

Cuteness: You may laugh at this, but it's entirely serious. You love anything that is cute, you love being cute, and you see the cuteness in others. Cuteness touches on human tenderness. *As a leader, you will be able to see multiple sides of people, beyond prowess and competence. You appreciate their "soft" or "cute" skills. This is part of kind heart leadership.*

Celebration: As I was preparing to give this book my last pen strokes, a word came to me, as the words that have paved my life often do. The word was CELEBRATION. It made precise and complete sense that the last word of the C-Suite be "celebration" for two main reasons. First, the Empath, when at their best, most shiny self, gleefully celebrates. Yes, *gleefully*, celebrates themselves, others, and life. The *true* Empath will celebrate with you and for you.

Second, it is time to lead by celebrating. *As a leader, you are no longer here to trauma bond or to suffer until there is no more suffering. You are here to embody trauma rising and post traumatic growth through celebration.* As my co-author and publisher, Kayleigh O'Keefe, declares as a leadership principle: drink in the elixir of life. And to that I say, shots, shots, shots!

The pièce-de-résistance, at the center of it all and anchoring these spokes on the wheel, is **CHOICE**. *For the empowered Empath Leader, discerning and executing their choice, and creating spaces where others can choose, carries exponential meaning and ripples.* For humanity, choice is freedom. When the human can choose, the human is free. The enthroned Empath is a freedom fighter, freedom sharer, and freedom giver.

Leadership and The Rise of The Meek

Know the Empath C-Suite because these are your core characteristics. It will embolden how you walk in the world, as well as provide you with a template for who you want to work with, love with, live with, and travel with!

Let's Reflect on Your Mission

It is now time to ask yourself: *What is my mission? What am I here to do on the planet?*

Let me take some pressure off. You don't have to be the activist of all things or the innovator who creates something that changes history. The choices are many, and they all have impact and are profound. You may choose to be the one in your place of work who decides not to gossip, who values the energetic messages from the silent employee, who decides to embody a new way of being, not doing. You can also be that mold-breaking CEO who shakes the fabric of your company, your firm, or your entire industry. There is room, and great need, for all of us Empaths.

Parts of the Body

We are parts of the body. Each of us has a function, and we honor those functions. Each of us is working on a particular planetary grid. The grid is the people around us, whether you are in the banking industry or leading a global nonprofit. Maybe it's the political world. Maybe it's movements for Black and Brown Indigenous people, the LGBTQ+A communities, the safety of our beautiful children, or respect for our fur creatures. It doesn't matter. It might just be your family, but remember, once it starts—and no matter where it starts—it causes a ripple. The work that I

Claudia Cauterucci

am not doing, you are doing. We thank and honor each other for the parts of the body that each of us fulfills.

Don't ever doubt that you're causing a ripple. You've been causing a ripple all along; as an Empath, you've seen things, you've spoken things, you've shifted things, or you are the one in your family that did something different. Whether you left your home or whether you started a new lifestyle, you were the one in your family that has already started the ripple. So all I am saying is, let's do this consciously.

Ask yourself: *What am I here for? What do I consciously want to do?*

Ask the deeper questions, and don't worry if you don't get an immediate answer. Some of you will, some of you will not. Don't worry. Once the questions are asked, you'll start to see the signals and the answers. Sometimes they're very subtle. Sometimes they're plain as day.

Some ways to identify the answers is through the life force that just fills your body. It feels like a passion. It feels like goosebumps. It feels like: "This is ME! This is me. This is what I want to do. This is what fits." It also feels like: "I like myself here. I really like who I am when I'm like this."

All of those are signs of alignment.

Just knock on the door. What makes you feel completely alive? That is your life urge.

My mission is that I believe that everything begins with me. Harmony begins with me. Love begins with me. Politics begins with me. And when I mess up, which is on a daily, repair begins with me.

Leadership and The Rise of The Meek

I create blueprints, chart pathways, and partner folks on their journey home to themselves, to their whole self.

The Empath Leader training and this book are an invitation to come back to your giftedness, amazingness, and brilliance. Loving your human imperfection is essential too. Come home, Empath. Come home, human.

Chapter 12
My Own Empath Leader Story

"Out beyond ideas of wrongdoing and rightdoing, there is a field. I'll meet you there."

— Rumi

I come from a lineage of social justice activists. My dad was a Kennedy die-hard and an early Peace Corps volunteer deployed in Colombia, where he met my mother. My parents were both leaders in their own right and are still joined—and remain in love with each other—by their shared beliefs in helping others. They expressed this all their lives via their careers, volunteerism, what they read, what was discussed at the dinner table, and who they brought into our home.

Today, my parents are both in their 80s and still march for immigrant workers (with signs!), go to evening meetings about affordable housing, show up to rallies to represent "in numbers" the need for mental health in low-income neighborhoods and speak up for incarcerated juveniles. Before the pandemic, they spent one night a month in a homeless shelter responding to people's needs and translating for Latino and other immigrants. Now, at 82 and 83, they visit people in hospice, read them books, play them music, paint their nails and brush their hair, and show the Monday afternoon movies.

They also embodied the inner work. When their marriage was on the verge of total destruction and unprocessed trauma was spewing all over our home, my parents sought counseling and mentorship. They studied themselves and through progressive Christianity, became meditators. Their dedicated meditation practice—or "los veinte" ("the 20" silent minutes twice a day)—love affair with Jesus, and commitment to the inner journey, was a game changer in our home. They upleveled and pulled us up with them. They modeled trauma and also trauma rising.

It All Begins With Me

What I most learned from my parents, unbeknownst to them and to myself, in the silent yet intensely infusing way that energetic experience embeds, is that it all starts with me. Our family dinner table seated the complete range of economics, education, race, ethnicity, politics, and sexuality. Our dinner table—the most beautiful metaphor possible—was my most memorable schooling in Empath Leadership. The dinner table, our humanity, is made up of all of us, and we can break bread together no matter if we disagree. Conversation and respect were our portals to creating *one world*.

Speaking of the world, my father's career had us traveling all over the globe for the first 30 years of my life. I attended

Claudia Cauterucci

two pre-schools, one kindergarten, two elementary schools, two middle schools, two high schools, and two undergrad colleges. Whoa, moving so much, always being the "new girl", acclimating to new cultural paradigms on the fly, chiseled my adaptive survival skills. My most prominent defense mechanism—using my Empath skill of reading the dominant energetic frequency—was popular leadership. I got busy quickly to excel in school, participate in group activities, and speak up often. I showed up.

Here is the list version of my leadership trajectory, sneaky as it was, which mostly came to me through organic leanings, valence, and being chosen by others:

1. In Honduras, in first grade, I would arrange all my dolls against the wall, and teach them with a small blackboard, walking back and forth in front of them, speaking gibberish out loud. In the 4th grade, I presented a science project on pollution. This was the '70s; pollution was everywhere, but not yet trending.
2. In Panama, in 6th grade, I was chosen to read to the kindergarteners at lunchtime, and I had no idea that was a prestigious commendation. I just felt mature. In 7th grade, I was chosen as campaign manager for the elected school president based on my popularity, not my political fervor.
3. In Fairfax, Virginia, in the 8th grade, I was awarded "Best All Around" with my very first love, John Brody, the history buff and captain of *all* the sports teams. I'll never forget that day, not only because I walked hand-in-hand on stage with him but because I had just moved to the United States

a year prior. I still spoke English with a slight accent, and there I was, on stage with John Brody.

4. In Honduras, again for 10th grade, I performed in Honduras and Guatemala with the drama troop; was chosen as captain of the cheerleading squad based not on proficiency but on my willingness to take leadership; and for my senior thesis and under my father's recommendation, I went by myself to live for a month in a refugee camp on the border of Nicaragua during the Sandinista upheaval, clear that it was historical but unaware that it might be scary.

5. At my Pennsylvania Quaker boarding school for junior and senior year, I was selected as a peer counselor, was R.A. for my hall, and played the lead in a few school plays. It was through the Quaker Meeting for Worship that I learned the importance and joy of silence and the reverence for "being moved by the spirit."

6. In college, aside from serving tables at a pizza joint, I read books in Spanish to the blind and took notes in class for students with cerebral palsy. This was truly a heart calling.

7. In my early 20s, post undergrad, I joined a Washington, D.C., progressive and social justice Christian church. It was through their school, *The Servant Leadership School*, that I learned about the meaning of the inner and outer journey. I have never been the same.

8. As a satellite initiative, I was part of a small group that spearheaded a multicultural, inner-city church called *The Festival Church*. I was the Latina representative, and I created monthly

services and provided sermons in English and Spanish. That church continues today, attended still by some of my favorite spiritual co-travelers, including my parents. I was also in a racial reconciliation mission group composed of Black, White, and Indian men, and myself, the only woman.

9. In the mid-90s, also in Washington, D.C., through *College Summit*, a non-profit that aids inner-city teens with the college application process, I mentored inner-city high schoolers, and I later became the Workshop Director for their programs. I am so proud and thrilled to say that a few of the teens I mentored have now become Dynamic Meditation experts and Empath Leaders. I now collaborate with them on their leadership endeavors. Full circle bliss.

10. Lastly, I can't leave out what I describe as my Jerry McGuire moment, where I woke up in the middle of the night with an idea, not unlike the Dynamic Meditation Method and the Empath Leader. I nervously asked a group of parents, all friends with whom I had raised my son since kindergarten, to join me on a project I called *Project I Am 13*. The premise was to ritualize their 13th year, simulating traditions all over the globe and the Jewish BarMitzvah, to highlight their passage from childhood to adolescence. Every month for that entire school year, I asked one volunteer parent to teach them a life skill. The teens learned about stock market investing, how to prepare a full course meal, how to change a tire, and how to interview, amongst others. I gave them a workshop

on meditation. The *Washington Post* got wind of it, came to a few of our events, and wrote a Sunday article on it.

Leadership matters, even when unassumed.

Dreams, Figuratively and Actually

Despite all of what I just shared with you, leadership was not something I ever wore officially until now. I put it on. I sit on its throne. I teach it.

In 2009, I woke up from a dream that read, in huge capital letters with neon colors, the word DYNAMIC. The nonverbal but clear message that is typical of most dreams, was that it was time to gather and organize the best of all my tools, techniques, and processes that I had used over the years for my own self-exploration, self-healing, and self-expansion. In 2010, this became the Dynamic Meditation Method.

In 2020, as I was getting whiplashed by my emergent buried trauma and windswept by yet another wave of spiritual awakening, I began designing Wealth from Within, an idea to have a psycho-spiritual monthly roundtable where nothing is taboo and all things prosperity were to be discussed multi-dimensionally. Again, I woke up from a dream, and this time the words were EMPATH LEADER. Not empathic leader, not a leader with empathy, but Empath Leader.

After following Amanda Flaker's work on YouTube and deep diving into the expertise of renowned Empaths, such as Dr. Judith Orloff, Wendy Da Rosa, Anita Moorjani, and

Claudia Cauterucci

Lee Harris, who taught me, with great relief, to understand myself as an Empath.

If I can now piggyback on their trail-blazing work, I now identify as an Empath Leader, and these post-pandemic times called me. I began to implement my dream of Empath Leadership and called others.

Let Me Introduce My Co-Authors

In early 2022, I created the Empath Leader Training curriculum and held my first cohort in the fall of 2022. Kayleigh O'Keefe, Charles Martinez, and Carmen Berkley were in cohort one, and Felicia Ortiz was in cohort two, in the spring of 2023.

The individuals in the cohorts are either invited or interviewed to be a part of the cohort only because they need to align with the most functioning psychological stage of the Empath, the Authentic Altruist. Imperfect as well as geniuses, coming from all walks of life and leading in completely different areas, they all share a similar intense healing and self-empowerment journey.

You can read about their professional bios and get to know their strengths and vulnerabilities from their chapters. I'll just share where I feel intimately connected to each. With all of them I've done some trauma-rising coaching in some capacity.

* * *

Kayleigh O'Keefe and I spent a year in a women's mastermind group together, but it wasn't until we walked

My Own Empath Leader Story

through a small, ancient village in Italy that we really *saw* each other and joined in our reverence for life and God. There was no turning back. Since then, Kayleigh not only joined the E.L. training but she has spearheaded the creation of this book. What I most adore about her is her commitment to soulful excellence; she truly embodies the name of her publishing company.

Kayleigh doesn't just love life, she relishes in it, tasting every moment, documenting and studying herself in it, making love to it, and bringing God along. Just visit her Instagram or read her newsletter—you'll see what I mean. Kayleigh, through Soul Excellence and called by Spirit, has paved the way to this new earth via her roster of authors and books. Once you read the titles of the books she's published post-pandemic, you will see that she's been on the pulse of this great shift all along. She's the real deal. I am so proud and frankly honored, to be alongside her name in this book. Kayleigh is the absolute embodiment of the C-suite.

* * *

Charles Martinez is literally my longest-term relationship since we have now known each other for 22 years. We have physically, psychically, and spiritually traveled together. Charles and I have a memory book of laughs, cries, fights, and repairs that have coalesced into a securely attached adult relationship. Charles is an inner and outer circle friend since we're both just as much up for a night of salsa dancing as we are for a deep dive on Jungian shadow work or Brene Brown's vulnerability encouragements.

As a cherry on top, Charles and I have moved into the collegial world together as we are both holistic healers and psychedelic psychotherapy practitioners. As both profound friends and colleagues, Charles and I have embodied the trauma surviving and rising journey. Lastly, he is unofficially the president of my fan club since he has now taken all of my workshops, classes, and training, and we are both the better for it. Charles heals through his gaze alone. His presence in my life is a balm for the wounds in my root chakra. I adore him.

* * *

Carmen Berkley and I met during the pandemic on a podcast she was co-hosting with Richard Fowler, our point of connection. We did two podcasts where we had powerful discussions about trauma and anxiety, and we discussed themes merging people of color and their relationship to psychotherapy and meditation. Our conversation was on the pulse of the great shift as our communities of color were bursting forth into trauma rising, unapologetically releasing ancestral and systemic censorship. "It was *deep*," as Carmen would say. Unbeknownst to us, we were paving the way for our work as Empath Leaders.

Carmen and I connect in our experience of trauma surviving, ranging from our family of origin and our culture, all the way through systemic narcissism. In spite of it, we unequivocally and unabashedly believe that our wounds are our gifts. We count and claim community as an inextricable part of the healing journey. Carmen's work always has had communal upliftment as a principle, but it's Carmen's *beingness* that is her true shine. If there were a human picture for the flaming, kind heart, it would be Carmen Berkley. *She is fierce.*

My Own Empath Leader Story

* * *

Felicia Ortiz and I met through Charles, both natives of New Mexico, the Land of Enchantment. Felicia is ALL leader, whether in a group of friends, sitting on a board, running her business, or riding shotgun in the car. She is a natural and compelling leader and the exact embodiment of kind but firm. Felicia and I are most joined in that we laugh out loud as spontaneously as we tear up at what makes us feel deeply. We also speak fiery Spanglish with each other. What is most energetically available about Felicia is her heart, which is populated by the children of the world.

Felicia's life purpose is the children of this planet, and I am honored, thankful, and tearful that she has taken up her staff and walked a long, personal road to be an ally and advocate for them. Felicia is the part of the human body that I don't do because of my bleeding Empath heart; she has suffered and is witness to children's trauma in real-time. The healing, well-being, and evolution of children is where she anchors herself. Along with being a highly successful entrepreneur, Felicia is a tireless—and now trained—lightworker of endless capacity for children. I thank you.

Are You Ready for Empath Leadership?

Still asking yourself if you are an Empath Leader? Maybe parts of this journey so far have lit something up inside you. Keep following those as you read the wise words of my co-authors. For now—in this short version of the criteria I believe the world needs in an Empath Leader—see whether you discover alignment with these descriptors:

Claudia Cauterucci

You are a bridge-builder, whether you've noticed it or not. You make friends from different groups, with many types of people, and you are curious about others and their ways, even when your tribe of origin is not interested in that type of expansion at all. Your urge is to sit with others at the table, from all walks of life.

You tend to be an equal-opportunity friend. Most are invited to your gatherings, but things can get awkward because even though you get along with everyone, they might not get along with each other. Your urge is to bring together through points of connection.

You've done or are doing the deep-dive work to heal. Your urge is to be better—not competitively but because you can't help but reach for growth.

You want to stop or alleviate suffering, and you want healing for others but from a platform of joy. You understand that your wounds can transmute into your gifts. Your urge is to stop trauma bonding altogether and promote others where they shine.

You believe that we can start over no matter your past. Your urge is to endlessly strive for a better tomorrow, and can't help but walk towards it.

You believe that the well-being ripple emanates from you, not from others. You understand that your ripple is an inside job, and you're willing to do it. You can't bear the incongruence of helping others without having your house in order first.

The urge is for transparent coherence and congruence between your internal world and your external actions.

My Own Empath Leader Story

This is one of the hardest ones for Empaths, but it is the final criteria that moves you into leadership: You understand that hiding, making yourself small, or succumbing to fear no longer will do. You MUST anchor and shine in your gifts, not deplete or give them away. You understand that by BEING YOU in your genius, you are giving others permission to do the same. You are providing a mental model—an embodied paradigm if you will—for others to trauma rise and thrive.

Empath, I use this helpful phrase that activates rather than triggers you into emerging: **You are not showing off, you are showing up.**

As Pink Floyd sings, "Shine on, you crazy diamond."

Meet Claudia Cauterucci

Claudia Cauterucci is a psychotherapist, bestselling author, and internationally recognized as an intuitive, trauma-informed speaker and founder of her unique psycho-spiritual curriculum, *Dynamic R-Evolution*. She inspires trauma survivors, empaths, public figures, creators, and entrepreneurs towards getting what she calls "a multidimensional PhD on themselves."

Multilingual and multicultural, she helms a therapy practice in Washington, D.C., and provides a 12-week leadership training for C-Suite, creatives, and influencers called The Empath Leader, a program she specifically created in response to post-pandemic global socio-political shifts and places the Empath in a prominent role.

Claudia is also the producer and host of her podcast, *Heaven on Earth*, where she highlights the ways her guests are adding dynamic solutions, intimacy, and healing for the evolution of our planet. Claudia identifies as a Colorful person rather than a person of color.

Website: www.ClaudiaCauterucci.com

Part Two
Stories From Empath Leaders

Chapter 13
Your Sacred Rebellion
Kayleigh O'Keefe

"Welcome home."

These were the kind words uttered to me by the woman sitting next to me when I returned to a meeting of Alcoholics Anonymous for the first time in almost ten years. My heart sighed with relief as I embraced the truth of that phrase with a deep knowingness. I did feel at home. I felt safe, seen, heard, grounded, and connected.

As an Empath, those feelings are the exact needs I have always longed to satisfy. Even my struggles with alcoholism are a reflection of an unhealed Empath's drive to navigate the world without being overwhelmed by it entirely. Of course, it's not just me who craves authentic connections and experiences that ground me. Empaths, as you have learned in this book, are humans. You are an Empath, and so am I. I see you, and I'm here to tell you that our time has come to return home to ourselves. The world needs those of us who are called to leadership to step forward more urgently now than ever before. And in this chapter, I want to offer five principles for Empath Leaders.

But first, I'd like you to consider one model for building a more whole world–a model that has been right before our eyes all this time. It deserves a closer look.

A Blueprint for the New Earth Hiding in Plain Sight

Since my "return home" to Alcoholics Anonymous, I've come to wonder if recovery rooms around the world are the very blueprint on which to build new cultural and societal institutions. Twelve-step recovery rooms the world over offer the Empath - and, by extension, the human being - a blueprint for living. For those of you who are not familiar with AA or other 12-step programs such as Al-Anon for families of the alcoholic or Narcotics Anonymous and so on, there exists within AA, I believe, simple codes for living.

Connection to a Higher Power: In AA, members "turn our will and our lives over to the care of God, as we understand Him." Empaths, by and large, are naturally attuned to spirit and feel a deep connection to all beings. Imagine if each person in the world surrendered to the will of a Higher Power and, as a result, sought daily guidance from beyond the rationalizing mind.

Principles Over Personalities: I admire how twelve-step programs commit to "principles before personalities" and believe in anonymity as the great equalizer and spiritual foundation. Modern society practically demands that we put "personalities before principles," making it nearly impossible to engage in deep value-based conversation.

When everything is so personal, a question about an idea or a consequence becomes interpreted as a personal attack, and we cannot heal and move forward. Empaths, by our nature, have a deep love for all of humanity, and at the same time, I believe, at the authentic altruist level, operate from a clear set of personal values and virtues that enable us to take a higher perspective when it comes to both conflict and connection. We don't write someone off who does not agree with our opinions. And we don't keep people around out of obligation who consistently violate key principles of respect and the kind heart.

Sponsorship and Community: In recovery, members are asked to get a sponsor, a fellow alcoholic who has worked through the 12 steps and continues to practice the principles in all of his or her affairs. We cannot walk the path of life alone, especially as deep-feeling Empaths. Otherwise, we will easily get swept up in the narcissistic haze. Let this book be an invitation to find fellow Empaths and connect.

Prayer & The Power of Group: My heart soars in AA, where we often stand up at the end of a meeting, lock hands, and recite the "Our Father" or "The Serenity Prayer." I can feel our vibration rise in real-time as we express our gratitude for our daily bread and our hope for the future. Our hearts and breaths synchronize, and for a moment, we feel that deep sense of connection to God, ourselves, and our fellow humans.

Secure Attachment: The very structure of AA offers secure attachment to adults who often grew up without it. The meetings are one hour long, follow a set format that the chairperson leads, and invite people to share for 3-5 minutes only about their experience (not their opinions) as it relates to alcohol and alcoholism. Each share is a treasure trove as I listen to others - and myself - navigate the complexities of emotions and the inner world. I fall in love with humanity every time I hear someone share how they are attempting to navigate a challenge in life without taking a substance to numb out the pain. They are being fully human.

Perhaps Alcoholics Anonymous is the greatest global example of "turning fault lines into gold mines." Perhaps since its founding in the early twentieth century, AA has been unknowingly paving the wave and offering a blueprint for the rest of humanity in a post-pandemic, fear-based, disconnected society to now follow. Imagine more and more people gathering in person to share their experience, strength, and hope with each other in rooms where there are no dues or fees, no leaders, no power plays, no mascots, no political activism, no specific goals, no dogmatic belief systems, and instead fellowship and communion. New earth structures like recovery groups are all around us once you open your eyes and your heart to perceive them.

When Empaths Abdicate Leadership

I've come to believe that many Empaths struggle with addiction precisely because they have abdicated their calling as leaders. Have you ever ceded your natural instinct to lead in favor of a dominant energy or stronger voice in the room? Have you easily backed down to someone who has come across as strong and sure even when you knew that you were picking up on something that needed to be spoken to?

Your Sacred Rebellion

I'll never forget sitting in my swanky hotel room in Beverly Hills alone after hosting a successful book launch party with twenty women in business who had flown in from all across the country. Just hours earlier, I had stood at the front of the reception and called each author up by name and shared a personal story as they received a copy of their book. It was a touching celebration, and the photos that commemorate that day reveal the pride and joy the authors felt about our collaborative effort. But when the crowd disappeared, I felt trapped in my own despair, like I had given everyone my all, but no one could see me or hold me. I drank a bottle of brut champagne, ate the rest of the specialty cake, and hoped to never wake up.

Because Empaths seek group harmony and cohesion and deeply value respect for their fellow man, they have often shrunk themselves to make space for the most domineering personality. The Empath steps down, and often, the narcissist fills the void. This has ramifications for the collective, yes, but more importantly, it robs the individual Empath of fulfilling his or her deep calling to create the new earth. Trapped in this pattern, the Empath's star starts to fade, and her energy wanes.

The old earth paradigm that the Empath must break out of in order to spiral up out of addiction is that of abdicating leadership to the dominant energy in the room. This is the wounded Empath's greatest saboteur, caused by a program that has put other people on a pedestal while ignoring their own brilliance. Leadership requires responsibility, and for recovering Empaths like me, this can feel scary or exhausting because we've felt overly responsible for everyone's feelings and opinions throughout our lives. But once we recognize our true nature, we can start to invite in roles and responsibilities that form an infinite loop of expansion as we give our leadership gifts and receive more of what we value.

Spiritual Reconstruction and Self-Care

As you have read in the opening chapters discussing the traits, gifts, challenges, and needs of the Empath, you have learned that self-care is not optional. It is a necessary, daily way of restoring your energy, and it has nothing to do with getting a massage, although they are amazing! In recovery programs, I believe, self-care sounds like this line:

"What we really have is a daily reprieve contingent on the maintenance of our spiritual condition. Every day is a day when we must carry the vision of God's will into all of our activities."

As Empaths, our spiritual condition - our conscious contact with a Higher Power in meditation, nature, service, however you deem fit, gives us the firm seat of our throne on which to sit and be guided by the spiritual realm as we take the lead to build a new earth. As sensitive Empaths, it is so easy for us to get agitated by the outside world and all of its unconscious behavior. Whenever you are feeling disgruntled, unsettled, or even just unsure, it is the perfect moment to consider how conscious your contact with God, spirit, the universe, and your Higher Power in that moment. When was the last time you closed your eyes, felt into the body, and asked for clarity? You are a powerful receiver of whispers and insights from the subtle realms all around us, but your daily self-care is your regular tune-up to welcome in the guidance so readily available to the attuned Empath.

Your Sacred Rebellion

I believe that the entire world is in need of a recovery program, and I believe that it is Empaths who are not only most aware of this, but also most ready and willing to take the necessary action to pave the path to a new earth. As noted early on in the Big Book of Alcoholics Anonymous, "Yes, there is a long road of spiritual reconstruction ahead. We must take the lead." I believe this fits for us Empaths. We are the bridge builders to the new earth, and we lay the spiritual path brick by brick through our actions. We lead the way for ourselves, our families, communities, societies, and nations through this spiritual reconstruction.

Humanity has lost its way, and Empath Leaders are tasked with blazing the trail to a new earth.

Standing For Heaven on Earth IS the Rebellion of Our Time

I am not a rebel by nature. Far from it! I've always loved following the rules. I don't like to whisper in church, I always use my turning signal even if no one is around for miles, and I love a good, orderly line. More than that, I've sought to represent institutions and uphold traditions that I believed existed for the purpose of group harmony. It's why you would find me sitting in the front row of the classroom or standing on the stage delivering commencement addresses for undergraduate and graduate ceremonies. But something happened in 2020. I suddenly realized that the people and institutions I had grown up trusting - and sometimes representing - did not share my core values of truth and wisdom. Suddenly, I had no choice but to rebel. I did not realize until learning more about being an Empath that I had been upholding a narcissistic system (whether in companies, churches, or communities), and now was my moment of rebellion. Rebel, I did.

I did not rebel by taking to the streets and raging at the world, but what I did do was start to focus on how I was being and where I was placing my energy. I observed how leaders in power used empathy as a weapon while disconnecting from the deeper, subtler truths of human connection and manipulating the people out of a desire for fear-based control rather than from a place of wisdom, prudence, and love.

My Empath heart ached during this period, and I did what I could with the tools that I had at the time to counterbalance what I was observing by beginning to build spaces for heart-centered leaders to come together and share their stories in books. I launched Soul Excellence Publishing.

My company's first book, *Leading Through the Pandemic: Unconventional Wisdom from Heartfelt Leaders*, was my way of creating and holding space for successful individuals to process the spiritual breakdown they were having, as so much was being thrown at them at once. I became a lighthouse for fellow Empaths to come home to a safe harbor and reflect on the challenges they were facing within their own hearts as the world tested their resolve and commitment to their integrity.

I kept following my intuition and putting out titles that spoke to what I sensed the world needed:

- *Significant Women: Leaders Reveal What Matters Most*
- *The X-Factor: The Spiritual Secrets Behind Successful Executives and Entrepreneurs*

- *Black Utah: Stories From a Thriving Community*
- *The Great LeadHERship Awakening*
- *STEM Century: It Takes a Village to Raise a 21st-Century Graduate*
- *The Diversity in Humanity: A New Vision for Creating Harmony in the Workplace*
- *The Queen Bee: Embody Your Truth and Lived Fully Expressed*

Only now, after training as an Empath Leader, can I look back and see how I have been following my sacred calling by creating spaces for fellow Empaths leaders to connect and co-create and putting out a vision for the future instead of a critique of the past. In May of 2023, in *The Queen Bee: Embody Your Truths and Live Fully Expressed*, I wrote:

> "The invitation to myself–and perhaps to you, dear reader–is to anchor in more fully to the vision for our kingdom. By anchoring into what is true, we elevate our honeybee into her fullest expression, The Queen Bee.
>
> As The Queen Bee, I am here to create a new kingdom, a new heaven on earth. I am for God, Universe, and I am for men and women of this earth who are also engaged in the work of evolutionary mastery, the work of creating more intimacy with self, others, God, and the planet for the fullest expression of our shared humanity."

While we may be sharing our individual stories in this book as Empaths, make no mistake, we are addressing a societal paradigm. You've read our description here as the lack matrix, a worldview that depends on beliefs around fear, scarcity, and "not enoughness" on all levels. Others describe it as the victim, aggressor, savior paradigm where we are on the lookout for the oppressed and oppressor, devaluating each other by the moment as we do. But for most people in the Western world, "it is what it is," meaning it's the reality of the society we are in, and things are presented to us in fairly black-and-white images: The egomaniacal but highly successful narcissist at the top and the rest of us "good people" doing the work to hold everything together. The truth is, these paradigms exist in our culture, institutions, and even close to home in our families, because Empaths are not recognizing their true gifts and not stepping forward as the kind-hearted leaders that they inherently are.

The principles I'm about to share—and really, this entire book—stem from an urgent need for action. As Empaths, our sensitivity and our kind heart give us the perception, strength, and conviction to create entirely new ways of being.

The 5 Leadership Principles for Empaths

You are being called to step fully into leadership. When we talk about leadership in this book, here we mean sovereignty of self. The word sovereignty means supreme power or authority. Sovereignty of self implies that we are seated on the throne of our kingdom. From this powerful vantage point, we engage in conversation with the Creator, and we align with allies who are building similar kingdoms.

Here are my five leadership principles for Empaths who are on this path:

1. Hold True to Your Standards
2. Anchor Into Your Leadership Frequency

3. Move From Problems to Possibilities
4. Drink In The Elixir of Life
5. Surround Yourself with Empath Leaders

Open your heart and see if what I am sharing resonates with your inner knowing about the moment we are in - and what is being asked of you.

Hold High Your Standards

We've all been there. You clarify your values and what you desire, whether in the form of a job offer, a romantic partner, or a new hire to your team. Then you realize that what you've signed up for isn't meeting your standards of excellence. Instead of holding true to those standards, the Empath in you thinks you might be being unreasonable, so you drop the standard. You say yes to clients that require so much motivation. You start thinking, "I could make this work," in a relationship instead of, "I am so energized by having this person in my life!"

Empaths, we must clarify our values and then hold to them energetically and in practice. If we do not, we sacrifice ourselves, and we continue to hold up the victim, aggressor, savior paradigm by being the savior who lowers their standards to over-accommodate. Clarify your values right here, right now, and create daily rituals that put those values first so that your very being emanates this new standard. Remember, if at any point you feel as though your standards are unreasonable, then what you are likely calibrating to is an external or societal standard and not the one that is naturally true to you.

. . .

Kayleigh O'Keefe

Anchor Into Your Leadership Frequency

As Empaths, it's encoded in our DNA to relate to one another. As we've discussed in this book, we are highly conscientious and aware individuals who can and do relate to people of all ages and walks of life. It's a beautiful part of our makeup. Driven by the desire for harmony, we often "drop" our energy to match the energy of the room. That said, when it comes to being a leader in your field or in your community, being relatable is hampering your influence as an Empath.

What is often happening here is that we are seeking to make other people comfortable by dampening our light and minimizing our accomplishments so that we do not come across as intimidating or perceived as "too much," "too big," or even just "too weird." This is a new realization for me personally, and here's what it will look like in practice moving forward: I will no longer be writing and posting all about my suffering, my healing, and so on in order that others can "trust" that I've "been there" and I "get it."

I have spent the last four years writing about and sharing these stories, and I am grateful to my younger self for doing so. She has helped me to clean up my inner world, reassess, and recalibrate toward deeper desires. Now, however, as a leader, it is time for me to stand fully in my magnificence and be comfortable owning what I've accomplished so much as the vision I hold for the future. That vision may be weird, unrelatable, or perhaps idealistic. It does not matter.

This is my sacred calling.

* * *

Move From Problems to Possibilities

Empaths are problem-solvers. We are fixers. We are therapists. We are healers. We see how any and everything can be improved and optimized because we believe in competence and collaboration. Again, this is a beautiful trait. However, there is a much better use of this heightened perception that we have in our leadership capacity. We must embrace the shift from seeing and solving problems to perceiving and activating possibilities. This is the paradigm shift we are advocating for in this book.

The shift:

- From the outer way to the inner way
- From creating from the past to creating from possibility
- From codependence to co-creation
- From lack and limitation to prosperity and abundance
- From illusion to truth

Empath Leaders, we must stay focused on this vision for a new earth, for heaven on earth, even as we are acutely aware of the problems that exist in the world today. In our highest leadership capacity, we are co-creating the new institutions that will enable human flourishing.

Drink In The Elixir of Life

It's common for Empaths to numb out and dissociate to deal with their feelings. Extra brut champagne and Trader Joe's Cookie Butter have been my drugs of choice throughout my life to numb my emotions and disconnect from the pain of reality. I believe that many Empaths turn to drugs and alcohol because we are so sensitive to the beauty of life, with all of its grief and joy. We actually get intoxicated by life.

Sunrises make us smile, sunsets make us weep. The smell of a flower turns us the f*ck on. The breeze against our skin energizes our being. We feel everything, and it is so beautiful to us. And yet, many of us have been shamed for these sensitivities, called sentimental and "too much" by the people around us. We turned to the more acceptable tools for living in modern society–drugs and alcohol–to disconnect from the heart and stay in the anxiety-inducing chatter of the mind. As an Empath Leader, it is time to purify the body, release the addictions, whether they be to substances, information, or habits, and get drunk on life, the raw beauty of it that you long to perceive but have abandoned to get by. It is time for all of us to surrender to our deep-feeling hearts and be a vessel for divine inspiration.

Surround Yourself With Empath Leaders

We must be around like-visioned people at this moment in time. We must find our Empath Leader tribe. Here we are! When we find ourselves over-explaining to friends and family or bending over backward to make exceptions for clients who can't match our level of responsibility or energy, we are doing ourselves - and our missions - a massive disservice. We are sieves letting our energy leak without abandon. Trust that you will come alive in the presence of other Empath Leaders. If only you could see what happens during Empath Leader training, how our eyes light up and our faces soften in each other's presence. We love connecting, learning, and co-creating. And now you are with us on this journey!

YOU are the Most Important Empath

In recovery, they say that the most important person in the room is the newcomer. The newcomer, just like a newborn, is a cherished reminder of the gift of new life and possibility. As you read this book, it is YOU who are the newcomer to Empath Leadership. YOU are the most important person in this book, you who are saying, "Yes, I AM an Empath, and I am not ashamed." And, "Yes, I AM a leader, and I am ready to stand firmly in my gifts." For too long, fear, guilt, and shame have muted the sensitive Empath's soul and driven him or her to small safe havens on the sidelines of society.

It is my hope that *The Empath Leader* becomes the leadership recovery text for the Empath in the same way the *12 Steps and 12 Traditions* have become the bible for those in recovery.

> May you see yourself in our stories.
>
> May you hone your gifts of intuition.
>
> May you lead yourself and, by doing so, show others the way.

Meet Kayleigh O'Keefe

Kayleigh O'Keefe is a USA Today bestselling author, speaker, and founder and CEO of Soul Excellence Publishing, the publishing house for Empath Leaders.

Sometimes referred to as a puppy for her endless energy, optimism, and playfulness, she is also quite serious about helping others reconnect to their soul, pursue excellence on their terms, and spark new cultural movements. Founded in 2020, Soul Excellence Publishing has published 17 international bestselling books featuring over 550 Empath Leaders from 16 countries across four continents.

Kayleigh received her bachelor's from Duke, an M.B.A. from the University of San Francisco, and has fifteen-plus years of experience advising Fortune 500 executives and building commercial teams at early-stage start-ups. She also hosts *The Future is Human* podcast, where she explores how to upgrade our human operating system so that we can experience deeper intimacy and connection. She leads by example, always allowing for her own expansion and seeking to master the inner game of life.

Kayleigh loves being an aunt and brings "aunt energy" to all of her endeavors, pushing the limits of what's possible and what's expected. She has walked over four hundred miles across two different routes of The Way of St. James pilgrimage through Spain and Portugal.

After spending most of her career in Washington, D.C. and San Francisco, she now lives by the beach in Hollywood, Florida, where she makes it a point to see the sunrise every morning, cultivate her yoga practice, practice tennis, and live by her values of inner harmony, being in nature, intimacy, vitality, and prosperity.

Websites:

https://soulexcellence.com/

https://kayleighokeefe.com/

Chapter 14
The Care Bear Model of Leadership
Carmen Berkley

D o you remember the 80s TV series *The Care Bears*? I should have been a cast member on the show. I basically thought I was the heart bear growing up. I have always cared a lot about people, and I have always been a highly sensitive person. If you were to ask my mother, grandmother, sister, aunts, or uncles who the most sensitive person in our family is, I am certain they would all very quickly point directly at me. I tend to cry on any occasion—I can't help it. Given my emotional nature, it's no surprise that I care deeply about the teams I lead. I used to feel uneasy about how much I cared for the people I managed, the communities I served through my leadership roles, and the advocacy I did to support them.

In my career, I have managed teams as large as 60 people and as small as two. I have always felt like I had an extra special connection with the people I worked with, almost like we were family members. At first, I couldn't quite put my finger on why. But then, I came across the term "empath" in a book about personality types. Even though I didn't

Carmen Berkley

believe I had any psychic abilities, as I learned more about the characteristics of an Empath and reflected on the meaningful relationships I had built with my teams, I began to identify with the sense of knowing and closeness I had with them.

My genuine concern for people is an inherent part of my nature. I listen to what people say and sense what they mean. I adjust my actions as a leader, facilitator, manager, or colleague to help people and teams unlock their full potential and achieve a high level of creativity and skill.

A key moment in my own leadership journey was my time as a Girl Scout. My mother's decision to enroll me when I was in the first grade shaped my life in so many ways. I remember feeling a sense of pride when I finally memorized the Girl Scout promise,

> *"On my honor,*
> *I will try to serve God and my country,*
> *to help people at all times,*
> *and to live by the Girl Scout Law."*

Picture me, decked out in my Brownie uniform, dutifully reciting the Girl Scout Promise with twenty other girls in unison every Saturday morning with our three fingers held high before going off to do our activity of the day.

Motivated by my eagerness to earn badges and a sincere dedication to being helpful, my experience transformed into something more profound. While I enjoyed collecting the badges and occasionally selling cookies to my neighbors, I enjoyed the camaraderie of being a part of the troop. I found my voice as a leader through the campfire songs, and

The Care Bear Model of Leadership

I was always the loudest voice, rallying our troops to get everyone back on the bus during field trips. My joy was building a community with people from different backgrounds who shared commonalities. It was one of the few places where working together and being highly motivated was not only accepted but celebrated. Let me be clear: We weren't just selling Thin Mints and singing songs. Earning badges was hard work, and the awards could not be achieved unless we were exceptional at what we did individually or worked together to achieve a group project. The Girl Scouts provided a nurturing environment where I developed as a person, explored my interests, and felt a sense of community with other highly driven young people.

The program taught me an invaluable lesson: If I continue to work hard, I could remain faithful to my authentic self – with my loud, funny, big personality – and still accomplish great things. It starkly contrasted with school, where I was often chastised for my joyful personality. In the Girl Scouts, however, my expressions of joy were celebrated, and I was seen as a leader because of them. The organization recognized and rewarded the unique qualities of every girl, whether they were quiet, athletic, scientific, or possessed another skill. It was a place where everyone's contributions were valued and where we were all encouraged to be our true selves. It taught me that there are different types of leaders who play different roles, and they must all be celebrated.

The Girl Scouts instilled three important lessons in me that have shaped my leadership philosophy:

1. **Be of service to others:** Whether being helpful to a bathroom attendant or a CEO,

providing excellent service to others is incredibly rewarding and I've learned to do so without expecting anything in return. The program encourages Girl Scouts to help people at all times, which reinforces the idea that everyone's needs are important. Treating everyone with the same level of respect regardless of their title or position is essential.

2. **Kindness is a powerful tool for leadership.** It costs us nothing to be kind as a leader, and it could mean everything to the people we lead. A simple smile, a friendly hello, and a warm disposition can go a long way in making people want to be in your presence as a leader. Have you ever met a disgruntled Girl Scout selling cookies? The answer is no because kindness is at the core of everything they do. While some Girl Scouts may be shy or introverted, you'll hardly ever find one who is mean or surly.

3. **Collaboration is key.** It's more powerful to build something with the community than to attempt to do it alone. While some tasks can be achieved independently, we can reach our larger goals and dreams more quickly, efficiently, and enjoyably when we work together. This is deeply ingrained in the Girl Scouts program, where leveling up is often connected to helping others in the community, volunteering, or learning new skills from a new set of people.

While each person in the program had their own unique qualities and leadership styles, our values of serving others

The Care Bear Model of Leadership

and treating people well remained the same. This is a fundamental aspect of the program and something we all learned to embody as we progressed. The experience taught me that organizations do not have to mold people into the leaders they want them to be but to encourage them to be their best selves and unlock their God-given talents so they, too, can earn their badges. I took these lessons and so many more with me into high school and college, and I continue to carry this sensibility into every job I have held since.

Being an Empath Leader means I view leading teams as a sacred gift. I consider management as an opportunity to cultivate deep relationships and take this responsibility seriously. Our intuitive spirit compels us to pay close attention to the people around us. We genuinely care about them as both team members and human beings. While my highly sensitive nature has sometimes felt like a weakness, and I have had to set personal boundaries, I believe that leading from a heart-filled space has allowed me to advance in my career more rapidly, unlock unique leadership qualities in the teams I have led, and impart knowledge to other highly sensitive, heart-centered leaders I have met along the way.

I've come to understand that being an Empath Leader means I'm not afraid to be intimate with the people I manage, and I'm not afraid of the word "intimacy." Of course, I don't mean intimacy in the romantic sense. But when we spend as much time with our colleagues as we do with our families or partners, there must be a level of intimacy that allows us to care for the people we work with on a human level.

If you're anything like me, you care deeply about leading your team and want to do it well. I can attest that our superpowers come in many forms, but at our core, caring for and building trust with our teams are the two most essential elements we must focus on to lead groups of people through complex work environments. If we want to drive our teams toward success, we must do so in a way that encourages them to unleash their greatness.

With that in mind, I wanted to share three ways Empath Leaders can use the power of care, trust, and community to build efficient, driven, and heart-centered teams.

#1: Approach with genuine care

My first job after college was a high-level executive position at a student-run education association in Washington, DC. In my first week, I could tell everyone was relieved I had arrived because the president of the organization was causing chaos due to his unpredictable and moody nature. I had to learn to manage a team of eleven people and earn their trust quickly.

I didn't have enough time to read all the books about leadership, and I certainly didn't have the experience to manage them. I remember searching online for "Best Companies to Work for in America" and coming across an article about Southwest Airlines. This article helped me refine my leadership approach. At the time, Southwest was known as one of the best companies to work for because of its emphasis on its employee-first approach. Despite being a smaller and quirky airline in comparison to its competitors, Southwest was achieving record-breaking profits, and the secret lay not in putting profit first but in valuing and cherishing its employees. This narrative resonated with me deeply. It wasn't just a story

The Care Bear Model of Leadership

about a thriving business but a testament to the transformative power of genuine care. Southwest Airlines' commitment to the well-being of its employees became a guiding compass for my own leadership philosophy. It reinforced what I already believed—that success is not merely a byproduct of achieving your strategic plan or hitting your profit margin; it's cultivated through authentic concern and a genuine prioritization of the people you lead. I was nervous to take the advice of a company that told jokes over the loudspeaker and did not have assigned seats, but if a giant corporation could care about its team members, so could I.

As I approached gaining the trust of this new team I joined, I knew I had a lot of work to do with each team member. I focused on building relationships with each person individually by taking them out to lunch, hosting dinners at my house, and having one-on-one meetings with them on a weekly basis. We had jam sessions in the office, birthday parties in the conference rooms, and we'd even grab cheap happy hours after work. Our organization didn't have the budget for relationship-building activities, but I believed that investing more time in my team members and prioritizing their needs would shift the energy of the workplace and make a positive difference. We would check in on team members who were sick and give them the support they needed. When someone's family member passed away, we made sure to give them extra time off. We did everything we could to make the team feel more like a community and less like a place where you just go to work for eight hours a day. With every job I have ever had, I go out of my way to sweat the details. I try to remember birthdays, anniversaries, partners' and children's names, favorite foods and sports teams, shoe sizes—any little tidbit I can to let people know that the boss is paying attention to their output and their life.

We need each other in the workplace to achieve our most tremendous success. It is important to be genuinely curious about your team members. To understand their likes and dislikes and take an interest in their needs. Not everyone may be interested in sharing this level of detail, and that's perfectly fine. However, I have learned that this is the currency we need when difficult situations arise at work. Team members need to know that their colleagues genuinely care about them and are invested in their well-being. When I talk about currency, I don't mean it in a transactional way; I simply believe it's vital to have currency with your team members and build good grace with them. This is especially true during intense situations (you will thank me later during budget, conference, or work planning season). As a leader, you need to have an actual relationship with your team members that includes care and curiosity to sustain difficult times. If there is genuine care and concern for each other, then you all have built up enough currency amongst each other for people to be able to use that currency to give each other the benefit of the doubt during turbulent times.

Investing in genuine care and curiosity paid off for us at the student association. One time, during a meeting with our board members in Miami, our executive team noticed that our paychecks had hit our bank accounts, only for them to bounce the next day. Understandably, the staff was very upset and extremely vocal about it. We didn't make a lot of money, and many people had automatic payments that were starting to bounce. Two of our staff members, the Organizing Director and the Legislative Director, who were both

The Care Bear Model of Leadership

Black women, came up to me privately and expressed their disappointment at the situation and how unacceptable it was for the organization to put them in that position. I agreed with them.

Getting paid was more than just a paycheck; it was about making sure they could pay their student loan bills on time, sending money back home to their family, and caring for ill family members. Without the close relationship we had built, we may have dragged our feet or waited for the insurance money to cover their paychecks. But I knew the stakes were high for these women, and they were counting on us as leaders to show up for them, especially given the excellent work they had done for us. While they had little faith in our chaotic president, I knew this was the moment for me to cash in the social currency chips I'd been earning with them to restore their faith in our leadership.

While we didn't have an immediate plan to pay them back, we wouldn't allow their financial situation to suffer because of an accounting error. At this moment, I had to use all the relationship currency I had built with my team members, hoping they would trust us enough not to quit, go to the press, or go to the board. We worked with the accounting team to identify exactly how the situation occurred, were honest with them about how the error happened, and found creative ways to give them resources so they wouldn't have to bear the burden of our organizational mistake. This approach helped us to keep folks on board as we laid the foundation to regain their confidence in us.

This experience taught me my first real lesson in using genuine care in leadership. There are times when we as leaders have to follow organizational policies and operate within certain frameworks, but it's crucial that we allow the parts of us that are human and caring to show up, too. When the going gets tough, we as leaders have an opportunity to use the knowledge we have gained through building relationships to make a better work environment and I believe we must do so.

Investing in authentic relationships and being curious about your team members' lives is about getting to know people and creating a stronger work environment. When people feel valued and supported, they are more honest and more likely to give their best effort. As a leader, showing that you care about your team members as individuals can inspire them to achieve great things together and help your team reach new heights.

#2: Be clear, kind, and truthful

As a people manager, it's become clear that many individuals have not had honest, straightforward conversations with their bosses about their leadership, skills, performance, growth, talent, or areas of improvement. Often, they are shocked to hear a dose of reality from me for the first time. My grandma Alma always says, "You catch more flies with honey than vinegar." So, when delivering constructive feedback to someone I'm working with, I try to do it in a kind, clear, and direct way. Beating around the bush doesn't help people grow or succeed. It's important to face the truth and work to improve upon it.

The first person at work who was honest with me was my office manager at the student association—a 60-year-old Black woman from Virginia. I had just become president of the organization, but I was still only 22 years old and new to

The Care Bear Model of Leadership

my leadership journey. Even at that young age and with little experience, the staff team treated me differently because of my title, and I probably acted that way, too. However, our office manager was never phased by titles or positionality. She had worked with celebrities, CEOs, and politicians, and as she would say, "they are all the same." She treated every person with respect, and she was truthful with them. Sometimes, she was unpopular with the staff team, but it was usually because she was honest with them about one of their shortcomings.

I appreciated her because I knew she had my back regardless of my title. She never let anything bad happen to that office, our staff, or me. She became our den mother and our home away from home. I could count on her to tell me if my hair looked ridiculous before getting on television or if there was an argument between team members while I was out of town and the issues still had not been resolved. There was a time I hired the wrong person, and she told me that I was making a huge mistake before I even made the hire. When I had to transition the person out of the organization a few weeks later, she held my hand and supported me through the process while lovingly saying, "I told you that person was not the right fit." She was the one person I could always count on for the truth. Sometimes, it stung a little, but growing up in a household full of truth-telling Black women, I knew the advice was helping to shape me into a better leader.

After my experience with the office manager, I knew I could earn the respect of the people I worked with by being honest with them. Over the years, I learned how to deliver feedback in a way that people could tolerate because not everyone is ready to hear the truth about their performance or how to grow to the next level. However, for those who are, I believe Empath Leaders have an innate ability to use the power of human intimacy to deliver positive and constructive information in a way that people can receive and sense. Since I have always had this natural talent, even in my youth, I felt right at home giving honest and direct feedback to people I supervised.

Even as a child, I was known for bringing humor, truth, and joy to difficult situations. My desire to seek justice for all has often led me to serve as the unofficial voice of the people when the community needs to get something done. In grade school, I was always the one to take charge. If we needed to advocate to get something from the teacher, I would do it. If someone in our friend group were mean to someone else, I would hold them accountable. If an injustice happened in the lunchroom, I would stand up to the bully. I had a natural ability to address difficult situations head-on and reveal the truth in people. Even if it was hard to hear, I could communicate it in a straightforward manner, and people would somehow accept it even if they did not like what I had to say. I have always been known as the friend who will "keep it real". While I did not love that title, I recognized the gift for what it is.

For me, telling people the truth is not just a choice but a deep-rooted need. I don't do it to put myself on a pedestal or to appear more pious than others. Rather, I do it because I believe people deserve to hear the truth from someone who cares deeply about them and is committed to honesty. There is a little fire that burns inside of my throat when I do not speak the truth. Although it hasn't always been easy, and I have certainly been accused of being too honest, harsh, crass, or offputting, I can confidently say that

The Care Bear Model of Leadership

every experience of being a truth-teller has made me a better leader. Honesty expressed from a place of sincerity is an essential leadership quality.

I must admit that being a truthful leader is a delicate dance. I haven't always been kind or strategic in my quest to be honest with everyone. I now know that it's equally important to have a lot of compassion, empathy, and mindfulness, especially when delivering feedback. While building trusting relationships with managers and peers based on unbridled truth has benefited me greatly, it's crucial to be clear about what parts of the truth are necessary to tell and the best approach for the person receiving the feedback.

As the civil, human, and women's rights director at a national labor federation, I had the privilege of leading a multicultural team of women who ran a national commission on racial justice. We had to produce a lengthy report that would impact millions of working people, and the stakes were high. I admired the intelligence, vibrancy, and skillset of a younger Black woman on the team. Especially her talent in strategy development, event planning, and logistics. She was my trusted right-hand woman, and I was training her to take my job.

Although I often praised her for doing well, one issue we were working on was her writing. Sometimes, she overlooked certain details, which was problematic since her work often went to the president or chief of staff of our organization, who often scrutinized the work that came from a department full of women of color. I spent hours cleaning up her work, which frustrated me. I believed the problem was fixable, and I was confident that she could turn things around quickly. However, when I received another document with the same issues a few days after giving her feedback, I became irritated. Was she not listening to my feedback?

In my frustration, I made a poor decision. I grabbed a red pen from my drawer and marked up her document in ink. I continued to do this with all her documents and left them on her desk overnight. I wanted to send a clear message that she needed to make a change in her writing *quickly*.

During a one-on-one meeting, through tearful eyes, this younger Black woman expressed how horrible she felt about the marked-up papers. I was just as horrified by my actions. While I had gotten my point across about her writing, I failed to build a trusting managerial relationship. I had not only broken her trust, but I had also broken her spirit. Instead of teaching or guiding her, I had just told her she was wrong. As leaders, we have to be direct at times, but as an Empath Leader I strive to have a level of connection with people that allows them to maintain their dignity during challenging conversations. I realized that her feelings and opinions were not only equally important to mine but also integrally related to what I was asking her to do.

So, I apologized and stopped marking her documents in red pen. We devised a better editing system, and her writing improved. Although we no longer work together, we are still friends, and she is a successful strategist known for how she interacts with and treats people through the work she does in the world. She taught me there is a way to be honest and truthful with team members without being harsh and hurtful. This aligns more closely with the leadership qualities of having a kind heart. Looking back, I realize my actions were not the best way to handle the situation. I should have

The Care Bear Model of Leadership

communicated more effectively and provided clearer guidance. Nonetheless, I learned from that experience and have become a better leader.

As I continued to grow as a leader, I sought out other leaders who shared my values of care in delivering information. That's how I discovered Brene Brown and her book *Dare to Lead*. I was stopped in my tracks when I read her quote, "Clear is Kind, Unclear is Unkind." I had to ponder each of those words and what it meant to be clear and kind.

Being clear as a leader means being direct, honest, methodical, and measured. Being kind means being empathetic, generous, and sympathetic. As leaders, we owe it to our teams to be both clear and kind to achieve our collective goals. Unfortunately, work environments often operate in an unclear and unkind manner, and Empath Leaders strive to break those cycles that do not serve our teams. Being clear and kind can be challenging but crucial for successful leadership. By communicating with clarity and empathy, we can create a work environment where individuals feel valued, respected, and motivated to achieve their goals.

As a leader in the C-suite, I strive to be someone my team can count on to tell the truth. Regardless of their position within the organization, I want my team members to know they can ask me anything, and I will provide an honest answer even if the answer is no. As a leader, our duty is to ensure that our team members are well-informed about growth opportunities, organizational policies, and how to move up or advance within the organization. I strive to be a leader who gives consistent feedback to colleagues and those I manage. A principle I hold is to provide consistent feedback year-round. I provide authentic feedback to those

Carmen Berkley

I manage and demystify it as being a bad thing. Leaders should provide reciprocated feedback so there are no surprises during annual reviews—that is how we build a culture of trust—no surprises and no unwritten rules when communicating with our team members.

People respond differently to feedback, and I have had to learn that there is no one-size-fits-all approach to delivering information. Some people may need more time to process feedback, while others may need more support or guidance to improve. It's important to remember that feedback should be given with the intention of helping the person improve and grow, not to criticize or tear them down. When we deliver feedback with empathy and kindness, people are more likely to be open to hearing it and to take it to heart.

Being a successful leader is akin to being truthful in any relationship; it requires a balance of honesty, compassion, and mindfulness. It's about being clear about what parts of the truth are necessary to tell and finding the best approach to deliver the feedback in a way that people can receive and grow from. As Empaths, we don't want to hurt anyone's feelings, but we also cannot run from telling the truth, even when it's difficult to express. I have learned to build long-lasting, trusting relationships with my team members through practice, mutual respect, and setting expectations and boundaries with colleagues where they have felt valued and motivated to achieve their goals.

#3. Co-create community and culture with your team

I must confess that I have always been the one who brings the fun. Even in summer camp, I was known as the arbiter of fun. I love playing games, karaoke, and being the first on the dance floor during the Electric or the Cha Cha Slide. I am also the fun auntie, so it makes sense that, as a leader, I strive to create a culture that fosters community, laughter, joy, and fun.

So it's no surprise that I see a connection between building a strong community at work in hopes of having a good time. We spend a significant amount of time at work. Some days, I leave for work when it's still dark outside, and I come back home when it's dark again, which means I have spent more than 8 hours at work. While I love the people I work with, I can't say that I love them more than my husband and family. However, I believe creating a sense of community and culture at work is essential, given the amount of time we spend there. Creating a community is crucial because some people on our teams may need or desire this sense of community because they have left their home community to take the job they are currently in. Some people may find joy or get energized from work, and it's important to cater to their needs as well. There may also be individuals who don't get joy or energy from work, and that's okay, too. Still, I believe that providing a sense of community and culture that team members are encouraged to engage with is a critical must because of the amount of time we spend at work.

I first recognized the importance of work culture when I worked for a national civil rights organization in Baltimore, Maryland. The membership-based, dues-collecting organization was more than 100 years old, the main office was housed in an old convent, the staff was spread out across the country, and at that time, Zoom did not exist, so most of the work was done via FreeConferenceCall.com or in-person conferences. It was crucial for our department to have a strong culture and a sense of community among us. I was on the field team, and they created a strong culture that made members want to be part of the organization, and they were paying their hard-earned money to work towards justice and freedom in the world.

My boss at the time was a reverend. He was exceptional at creating a sense of community and culture. He made each of us on the field team feel special. When he was with us as a group, he spent time training us, imparting knowledge, advocating with us and for us, and always had a kind heart and a listening ear. He also made time for us individually, and even when he wasn't available, he made us feel like he was always there for us, which gave us a sense of comfort.

The organization felt like a fraternity or a sorority, and we always had to wear a uniform, even though we did not have a formal one. Our boss took it to the next level by ordering us jackets and polo shirts with our names and the organization's logo on the front. He also ordered hats and scarves, which made us look and feel cool and unique. People wanted what we had but couldn't have it because they weren't part of our group. This sense of community was unbreakable.

The organization was unique because of its age and size, and it even had its own chant. Even today, if you ask anyone who is part of the organization what the chant is, they will be able to sing it in unison. There is a strong sense of pride and culture associated with being part of the organization, and even when you leave, you are still part of the family.

Creating that type of allegiance to an organization, building a community, asking people to convene in that way, learning a chant, and operating in a family environment takes a

The Care Bear Model of Leadership

special kind of leader. While some people may scoff at the idea of operating as a family at work, others would rejoice at the opportunity to participate in something special. Some leaders have a unique ability to tap into the human intimacy that pulls at other people's heartstrings. They remember small details that people care about, such as their favorite snacks, music, and books, and merge that with a highly curated, goals-driven agenda. In doing so, they are able to build amazing teams that achieve successful outcomes.

I have adopted this way of building teams and believe that operating in this way creates a sense of belonging. Although the pandemic has discouraged people from gathering physically, I still believe that most people yearn for a sense of community, even if it's online or over a text thread.

With every team I manage, I consciously think about the community we are creating. We develop community agreements and revisit them often. We have team retreats bi-annually or annually and allow multiple team members to present. I buy my team members gifts and take their needs and accessibility into consideration.

When I contract with an outside facilitator, I ensure that their values align with mine so that we can co-create the energy of the space together. While it's easy to have an entire retreat focused on strategic plans and goals, I make it a point to dive into the interests of the team members and do activities that reinforce their desires. I do this because I believe that even if I am the leader, we are building the ecology of the team *together*. I used to think this approach was silly, but honoring the ideas, rituals, principles, cultures, time, and skills of my team members has created stronger teams.

Carmen Berkley

Being heart-centered does not mean I am not goals-driven. I want our team to hit every goal, and I want us to do it on time. I have just learned that hitting key result areas to achieve data-driven goals is just as important as ensuring people feel good about the process. It's important that people feel a sense of achievement and connection to the outcomes, as well as recognition and rewards for their contributions. Leaders should recognize the areas of genius in their team members, create space for and validate those talents, and harness new talents they might not have even tapped into yet.

I have finally accepted that I have a gift of being able to see things in people that they cannot see themselves, and I must create a strong community and culture at work to foster safe environments where people feel comfortable enough to do their jobs, envision, and dream. When people feel safe, they are more likely to unleash their greatest powers and create. I now know that I gain the most joy when my team members receive credit for achieving their personal greatness—even more than when I am getting accolades for my own.

As I continue to progress on my leadership journey, fostering and protecting a community and culture within organizations, no matter how large or small, is one of the greatest things I can do. It ensures that my team members know that it's safe for them to do their work well and execute on their wildest dreams.

Before I let you go, I want to leave you with this:

Learning how to lead in this way has been about accepting my leadership style as a caring, sensitive, and truthful

The Care Bear Model of Leadership

person as a positive leadership style, not a weakness. I will always be the real-life Care Bear with the big hearty laugh, larger-than-life personality, and the gift of gab. I will continue to be a truth-teller and practice telling the truth, considering people's feelings.

I will keep buying cookies from every single Girl Scout I meet at the grocery store because of the impact that organization has made on my life. I will continue to value service, kindness, and collaboration, and I will always embrace them in my leadership philosophy as they have served me well.

If you resonate with anything that I said and feel like you are also a Care Bear with an overwhelming sense of wanting to protect the people you work with, know that there are other leaders out there like you. There is nothing wrong with your leadership style, and I encourage you to continue caring deeply about the people you manage and those in your orbit.

I believe that people who care deeply about others are special, and it takes a lot of energy to maneuver through the world with a kind heart. It is a gift to lead teams in this way, and people will benefit from your tenderness and be forever impacted by the way you took the time and had the courage to lead with vulnerability.

Continue to approach your team members with genuine care, and strive to be clear, kind, and truthful. This can be a hard one for us at times, but it's essential to master as it affirms the maturity of our leadership. Most importantly, we have a special ability to create beautiful spaces filled with community and culture that people want to be a part of.

Carmen Berkley

As an Empath Leader, you possess a special gift that is truly magical. It is even more fulfilling when you have the chance to manage, lead, or mentor others. Please know that your actions, no matter how small, are filled with goodness and kindness, and that is more than enough to make a difference in the lives of those you lead.

Meet Carmen Berkley

Carmen Berkley (she/her) is driven by the belief that communities are powerful entities that deserve to be heard, kept safe, well-resourced, and equipped with the tools to manifest their dreams—ultimately paving the way for racial justice, equity, and freedom in our lifetime. Throughout her career, Carmen has dedicated herself to shaping a future that uplifts powerful yet marginalized individuals through her expertise in advocacy, storytelling, communications, organizational development, and philanthropy.

Currently, Carmen serves as the Vice President of Strategy and Impact for the Inatai Foundation, spearheading policy and advocacy, communications, collaborations, capacity building, and grantmaking aligned with their enduring vision. In her role, Carmen oversees Inatai's annual grant-making, which surpasses $60 million, contributing to the transformation of racial justice and equity in Washington and beyond.

Carmen's impactful journey includes leadership roles at prominent organizations such as the United States Student Association, NAACP, AFL-CIO, Planned Parenthood Action Fund, and in political and executive leadership consulting.

Recognized for her outstanding contributions, Carmen has earned accolades such as Essence Magazine's Woke 100 and Washington Life Magazine's Top 40 Under 40. Her dedication to social justice has been acknowledged by her peers throughout her career. Carmen spent four years as a co-host and producer for one of the nation's longest-running women's radio shows on WPFW 89.3 FM and WOWD in Washington, DC.

Currently, Carmen holds significant roles as the board chair for re:Power, executive board member for the National Domestic Workers Alliance, Equity Advisory for Sephora, board member for Can't Stop Won't Stop Consulting, and she proudly serves as a founding member of BYP100. Carmen engages in creative endeavors in her leisure time, facilitates meetings, DJs parties, and attends concerts with her talented husband, Lee Anderson, and their dog King T'Challa.

Chapter 15
Human Piñata
Charles Martinez

"Charles, you're like a human piñata—a burst of treasures emerged from your trials."

Today, I believe this to be true. The aftermath of a tragic night in the spring of 2002 brought positive outcomes and a ripple effect of hope, self-discovery, acts of giving back, the art of forgiveness, and an enduring appreciation for life and the greater unknown.

The world perceives me as a decent-looking man standing at five-foot-eleven, with brown hair, a dark, groomed beard, and warm, inviting brown eyes. However, there was a period in my life when I couldn't even open my eyes. Both of my eyes remained swollen shut for weeks, and my head swelled to the size of a watermelon. My face bore the marks of deep bruises, concealed beneath bandages that had absorbed the traces of blood, fear, and evil. I lay in a state of utter helplessness for months, leaning on the combined support of a miracle, prayer, my dedicated medical team, and the unwavering love of my family and friends.

Charles Martinez

On an otherwise ordinary Saturday in April 2002, a man took a baseball bat and savagely beat me. The day had been filled with the joy of celebrating my father's 49th birthday, and the abrupt, senseless assault came without warning or provocation.

As I stepped out of my car and made my way toward a friend's apartment, I passed by a vehicle with two unfamiliar men inside. The driver shouted, "Hey, you! Where's Coleen?" It was an especially dark night, and I didn't recognize the car, the individuals, or the name, which left me feeling uneasy and apprehensive about engaging in conversation. My instincts, or claircognizance, screamed something wasn't right, but regrettably, I disregarded that inner feeling. Seconds later, I distinctly recall hearing a female voice cry out, "Charles, watch out!" When I turned to look, I was met with the horrifying sight of a menacing figure swinging a wooden baseball bat at my face. In the next instant, my world turned crimson as I heard a piercing, alarm-like noise in my ears, just like a scene from a movie where someone flatlines.

As I tumbled to the ground, confused by the sudden assault, I felt a barrage of kicks landing on my face, head, back, and stomach. Amidst the chaos, I sensed someone straddling my neck, but it wasn't my assailant; it was my beloved friend Felicia, my guardian angel, valiantly shielding my head from further harm. At that moment, my recollection became hazy as I disconnected from my physical body and found myself observing my suffering from an elevated vantage point. It was as if my out-of-body experience shielded me from the distress. The next thing I knew, I found myself standing in my friend's apartment bathroom, my face and hands covered in blood. I couldn't comprehend how I had ended up there, and I couldn't help but experience a mix of embarrassment and guilt for inconveniencing my friends. I sheepishly asked for a bandaid to stanch the bleeding, unaware of the severity of my injuries. In my confusion and pain, I pleaded with them not to involve the police or an ambulance, as I wished to avoid causing a scene. Looking back, it seems like an irrational request, a behavior characteristic of a true Empath, but of an Empath afraid of asking for help and to be seen.

Forgiving with Boundaries

In the Fall of 2023, I attended an all-men's meditation retreat for a weekend, where we probed into topics like balancing the divine feminine/divine masculine, free will, life and death, and how our past experiences shaped our present selves. That particular retreat helped underscore my burst of treasures, which contributed to helping me write this chapter.

Throughout my life, I've embodied a forgiving nature, perhaps to an extent that some might perceive as a weakness. Learning the importance of setting boundaries came the hard way as I navigated the complexities with family, friends, acquaintances, and people who were intentionally unkind. However, my assault brought a profound realization – the act of forgiveness towards my assailant was crucial, but it needed to be accompanied by intention and well-established boundaries for my sensitive and empathic soul.

As an Empath, I possess the gift of understanding other people's perspectives, even those of my assailant. After the assault and during the subsequent trial, I delved into his background and harbored compassion for the wounds he carried. The common challenge for Empaths, myself included, lies in extending understanding to others to the point of neglecting our own spirit and gifts. Balancing compassion with the necessity for personal boundaries became a struggle. I devised a blend of comprehension for his experiences and utilized labels to clarify his actions. This approach enabled me to create emotional space, facilitating a more rational processing of my feelings.

Instinctively, I ascended the emotional energetic AGFLAP (anger, grief, fear, lust, anger, pride) ladder. I was first introduced to AGFLAP through Claudia Cauterucci's Dynamic Meditation workshop, where she referenced physicist Lester Levenson's teachings from a retreat she attended called the Release Technique. The Release Technique is built upon Lester Levenson's principles, particularly focusing on releasing dense energetic emotions such as those encompassed by AGFLAP. Claudia found Lester Levenson's concepts and the Release Technique to be transformational, and these teachings have had a profound impact on me as well. Lester Levenson has authored several books, including *No Attachments, No Aversions* and *The Final Step to Freedom*.

Many of the core tools utilized in Claudia's Dynamic Meditation Method are derived from Lester Levenson's work, highlighting the profound influence his teachings have had on her approach.

Through AGFLAP, I transitioned from apathy to grief, then to fear, ultimately reaching a point of anger. My anger gave me permission that was a reflection of my own self-compassion. You see, society views anger as a negative emotion but it's your follow-up action that can transform that emotion as a climb to what Lester Levenson calls CAP (courageousness, acceptance, and peace). Anger itself can be a portal to self-knowledge if seen, validated, and understood. What ends up happening with Empaths is we deny our anger and don't look at it for its messaging.

I perceive anger as a signal, a trip-wire of information, indicating that a crucial message is on the horizon for an Empath. It's essential for Empaths to cultivate trust in their anger, because it often carries profound insights. Unlike others, Empaths tend to prioritize understanding various perspectives before acknowledging their own feelings, making it a lengthier process for them to validate their anger. However, the very nature of anger compels Empaths to reintegrate themselves into the equation. This process is instrumental in recognizing the significance of their emotions in a given situation. It grants Empaths the permission they need to acknowledge and embrace their anger.

During my healing journey, I found myself concurrently engaged with the justice system, seeking to prosecute my assailant. I seized the opportunity to deliver a victim's statement during his trial. Despite still grappling with anger at the time of the hearing, I channeled that emotion into passionate words that allowed me to express my sentiments toward him. These words ultimately played a crucial role in my journey toward forgiveness while also reinforcing the necessity of firm boundaries. This was my sacred pause, my permission to be angry. I expressed the following list of savage words to describe my assailant, which allowed me to reclaim my own sovereignty, a decisive move to regain control over my narrative:

Charles Martinez

Ignorant: I employ the word *ignorant* because I believe my attacker failed to grasp the full consequences of his actions. He likely never contemplated the arduous road to recovery that lay ahead for the person he had injured. My head swelled, my life confined to a hospital bed for nearly a month, my body contorted at a 45-degree angle for two long months. Basic functions became luxuries as I relied on bedpans for necessities and had nurses bathe me. I lay there, helpless and bewildered, unable to fathom why this nightmare had befallen me. For two weeks, my eyes remained swollen shut, and when I could finally face my reflection, I was terror-stricken by the brutal aftermath of that dreadful night.

Selfish: I use the term *selfish* because my assailant seemed fixated solely on causing harm that night, without any consideration for the rehabilitation that lay ahead. He failed to contemplate the toll this act would take on my family, both emotionally and financially, as we were forced to take time off from work to facilitate my recovery. He never paused to think about the countless lives disrupted and the enduring pain he inflicted on so many.

Aggressive: *Aggressive* aptly describes him because it appears he had never learned healthy ways to cope with his emotions.

Cold-hearted: I use the term *cold-hearted* because his brutality extended beyond a single blow; he continued to rain merciless kicks upon me as I lay defenseless on the ground, struggling to make sense of the harrowing situation.

Cowardly: And lastly, I label him *cowardly* because he chose to wield a weapon against me, striking me from behind without reason or provocation.

As I traverse my life's journey and lean into my Empath gifts, four beautiful treasures emerged from my human piñata experience:

1. I found the courage to come out of the closet and live my life authentically and unapologetically.
2. I've learned to heed the initial whispers of my intuition, paying close attention and actively listening to its guidance.
3. I remain committed to expressing gratitude for my ability to express my emotions as well as empathize with others, even those who have wronged me. Importantly, this gratitude extends to having increased compassion for myself.
4. Finally, I found my calling as a healer, and when treating individuals who have experienced trauma, I connect with them on a deep level—I feel them, see them, hear them, and can truly relate to their experiences.

I firmly believe that life experiences, whether inspiring or traumatic, have the remarkable power to shape our spirit and redirect the course of our lives. In my case, my assault was a needed turning point, one that I now view with pure respect and gratitude. I made the conscious decision to forgive my perpetrator long ago, recognizing that forgiveness is a crucial step in my healing journey. With forgiveness came a newfound sense of purpose and positive action which I now claim as an enormous victory. This surprisingly beautiful gift afforded me the opportunity to navigate life as a leader, a healer, and a visionary for my new heaven on earth.

Treasures Within

Have you ever heard of the religious term "Upside Down Kingdom"? The Bible states, "The greatest among us are those who serve. This is the upside-down kingdom of God. It is a kingdom where the "last will be first, and the first last" (Matthew 20:16). A kingdom where it is the humble who inherit the earth (Matthew 5:5) and the rich who are sent away empty (Luke 1:53)."[1] As an Empath, it was imperative to flip my upside down kingdom for my own personal healing, growth and to bring back my joy. But what did this mean, and how would I do that?

After recovering physically and continuing my emotional healing journey, the decision to openly acknowledge my true self was a daunting one that had haunted me since I was around nine years old. The prospect of being identified as a gay man filled me with terror and revulsion. Questions of whether I would be perceived as lesser or face rejection from family, friends, or my church loomed large. It took several years to summon the courage to reveal this truth to my family and friends back in rural Las Vegas, New Mexico. In my pursuit of living authentically, I intentionally confronted my apprehensions and officially embraced my true self. This process, an incredibly liberating experience, unfolded as a precious journey toward self-acceptance, self-worth, and self-respect. It was only at this point that I fully grasped the immense burden I had carried for years – the weight of guilt, shame, fear, and disappointment imposed by a societal, educational, and religious narrative that had ingrained itself into the core of my being.

Remarkably, it was my post-assault experience that served as a catalyst for overturning this false narrative. The profound realization that life can change in an instant, with no assurance of another day, felt surreal yet served as a poignant reminder of the importance of embracing authenticity and living with intention. On January 21, 2015, I met the love of my life, Carter, and it was love at first connection. After seven years of happily unmarried bliss, we joyfully transitioned into married life on November 11, 2022.

In addition, I consciously committed myself to giving back to society to serve folks who were ill. My aim was to make a meaningful contribution as a healer, leading me back to my academic pursuits to obtain a degree in the healthcare field. While I considered the path of medical school, I ultimately opted for a career in nursing. This decision was heavily influenced by the remarkable nurses who had been unwavering pillars of support during my recovery and the steadfast presence of my cherished family and friends. My choice to become a nurse was driven by a deep desire to engage directly in bedside care, forging human-to-human connections with those undergoing experiences akin to my own. I aspired to change the trajectory of my story, transitioning into the role of the empathetic, compassionate caregiver for those in need. In the end, it would serve as the motivating factor for my own healing journey and in maintaining a connection with my authentic self. Forging mutual connections, fostering balanced respect, and nurturing relationships with individuals who share similar experiences and values

Charles Martinez

would become my guiding strengths as I move forward in life.

I dedicated several years to working as a registered nurse in an acute hospital setting, all the while pursuing my master's degree in nursing to fulfill my ambition of becoming a Family Nurse Practitioner. The decision to return to school for my master's was driven by my yearning for greater autonomy in making medical decisions for my patients.

Upon earning my Family Nurse Practitioner license, I committed the following six years to serving as a Nurse Practitioner for a prominent healthcare company. However, when the coronavirus swept across the globe, I found my own physical and mental health on a steep decline. The demands of the crisis left me with neither the time nor the energy to care for my patients as I had once cherished. It was as if I was compelled to treat patients like objects on a conveyor belt undergoing routine inspections. My great love and passion for healing were fading, and it was a difficult and trying time for me.

At a crucial moment, divine intervention unfolded yet again when my dear and trusted friend Claudia Cauterucci introduced me to the realm of psychedelic-assisted therapy. Over the course of a year, I embarked on a profound personal journey, delving into the depths of my unresolved trauma and uncovering more of my hidden wounds and innate gifts. The convergence of my past, present, and future formed a beautiful tapestry of my existence. Throughout this transformative period, I confronted my past demons with a newfound sense of gratitude, kindness, love, and compassion. This process became a catalyst for healing old subconscious wounds, fostering reconciliation with loved ones I had once unintentionally hurt, and reigniting the empathic gifts inherent in my being.

It was during this profound experience that I discovered my true purpose, one aligned with my desire to assist others in their times of need who also had the burning desire to heal their trauma or expand their well-being. It became clear to me that my professional path needed to run parallel to my personal journey. Today, I provide care to patients who have chosen ketamine-assisted therapy as their preferred treatment for improving their mental wellness.

Divine intervention would step in once again when I chose to participate in the Empath Leader training. This course helped to unravel and refine many of my innate gifts. Among these, a profound ability emerged — the reawakening of "my clairs." For those unfamiliar, "clairs" encompass four psychic avenues: claircognition, clairvoyance, clairaudience, and clairsentience.

Claudia also coined the concept of clairsmelliance, which she and I recognized as a personal ability. While this fifth clair may not be found in conventional sources, it aptly describes my age-old capacity to perceive emotions through smell, and we've given it a newfound label. So many times I've found myself not "seeing red" as most people describe but "smelling red" when angry. In fact, the smell informs me that I'm angry before my mind does.

After the Empath Leader course, I've validated and honed this skill, allowing myself to associate specific scents with distinct emotions. For instance, anger is akin to a "reddened" burnt syrup. Happiness evokes the scent of coconut. Negativity carries a metallic aroma. The relationship between smell and emotion is well-established in psychology. It's known that certain scents can trigger memories or evoke specific emotions in people. My ability to smell emotions seems to be an extension of this phenomenon, where my emotions are accompanied by distinct olfactory sensations. While lacking traditional scientific validation, my clairsmelliant perception remains consistently accurate, offering valuable insights into my emotional states and aiding in self-awareness and emotional regulation. Have you ever experienced the sensation of smelling your emotions? If so, and you've struggled to articulate it, let me assure you, it's a genuine phenomenon. You possess the ability of clairsmelliance!

Reflecting on my journey, I recognized a consistent reliance on clairsentience and claircognizance during moments of peril or unease. Contemplating how my life might have unfolded had I heeded these intuitive signals more consistently, I ponder the alternate paths those discomforting moments might have taken. However, that's not what God or the universe had planned for me. Thanks to the Empath Leader course, I now regularly tap into my clairs, utilizing them in both favorable and challenging situations. Another valuable insight from this course was allowing myself to be angry without feeling bad about it and acknowledging gratitude in both the positive and challenging aspects of life.

Sometimes, life throws you curveballs, but if you embrace the concept of "turning your fault lines into gold mines," as expressed by Empath Leader alum Amanda Flaker, this will help you to pause for the possibility of what's yet to come. In addition, Claudia Cauterucci always expresses, "OWN YOUR PROWESS," and that's exactly how I intend to continue walking my path. I'm finally comfortable recognizing my inherent gifts and genius and overcoming my hesitation to be seen. This has been a challenging yet rewarding journey—but one that I am paving with gratitude. As I progress on my journey, I prioritize engaging in activities and connecting with individuals who ignite feelings of joy, curiosity, or contribute to personal growth.

As I now reflect on my entire existence and discern what truly matters, I'm truly grateful for my life's journey. I will continue to hold integrity for the four promises I made to God in the Spring of 2002 when he granted me wellness. Firstly, I resolved to forgive my assailant on my own terms. Secondly, I committed to embracing my authentic self by coming out of the closet. Thirdly, I pledged to give back and become a holistic healer and leader in my own right. Lastly, I vowed to embrace my kind-hearted nature with boundaries without ever feeling embarrassed or considering it a sign of weakness.

The next chapter of my journey begins with the realization that it's okay to be seen. This chapter marks the commencement of that transformative journey.

Meet Charles Martinez

Charles Martinez is a dedicated and passionate Family Nurse Practitioner committed to delivering exceptional healthcare, with a rich background spanning over fifteen years in the field. His educational journey commenced with a Master of Science in Nursing from Howard University, laying the groundwork for his career and leading to certification as a Family Nurse Practitioner.

Having initially specialized in cardiology and mental health, Charles' career took an expansive turn as he cultivated a deep interest in integrative health. This interest evolved into a true passion, drawing him to mindfulness-based practices, holistic medicine, and the transformative potential of psychedelic-assisted therapy—an inclination rooted in his personal experiences.

In his practice, Charles is dedicated to comprehensively understanding each client's unique needs and collaborating with them to achieve individual health goals. Grounded in principles of safety, reliability, and realism, his commitment extends to providing unbiased, high-quality care to every entrusted client.

Actively engaging with professional associations, Charles is a member of both the American Association for Nurse Practitioners and the Nurse Practitioner Association of the District of Columbia, fostering ongoing growth and connection within his field.

In addition to his clinical endeavors, Charles has earned certification in mind-body somatic practices. He extends his expertise as a holistic wellness coach, a role he fulfills alongside his position as Clinic Director at the Stella Center in Washington, DC. This dual responsibility allows him to seamlessly integrate a holistic perspective into his practice, empowering clients to pursue a path of balanced and comprehensive health.

In all aspects of his work, Charles' central focus is on empowering individuals to lead healthier, more fulfilling lives. He remains excited to contribute positively to the healthcare landscape and looks forward to sharing this transformative journey with you.

Chapter 16
Leading Education with Love
Felicia Ortiz

The Story I Was Born Into

How does a girl from the ranch who grew up in a mobile home end up becoming the President of the Nevada State Board of Education? It's a story of resilience, self-discovery, learning, and being guided by love! I was raised in a ranching community in northern New Mexico. My father was an electrician, and my mother went to college to become a teacher when my younger sister started elementary school. By society's standards, we were lower-middle class. I don't think I even realized that until middle school since most of my friends and neighbors were in the same boat. I was the kid who took tortillas with potted meat or burritos to school for lunch. One of my most vivid childhood memories is of our whole family sitting in our truck on a street corner in Santa Fe, waiting for someone to buy our truckload of firewood.

I am grateful for how my upbringing shaped me. I built my resilience and perseverance "muscles" early in life. I credit

Felicia Ortiz

our tight-knit small community and Chicano culture for instilling many of the values I hold dear today: respect, faith/spirituality, work ethic, integrity, and authenticity. When I was younger, the only thing on my mind was getting out and moving to a bigger city! Now I keep wanting to go back home...more about that later!

At the beginning of high school, I realized my way out was through education. I worked tirelessly to earn scholarships to pay for college, which was the only way I could afford to attend. My advocacy journey also started early in high school. I had resigned myself to being an introvert after being bullied badly in the eighth grade. I kept my head down and focused on my grades, and in the spring of my sophomore year, I was one of the "star" students in our bilingual education period. I was offered the opportunity to attend a conference organized by the University of NM student organization called MEChA (Movimiento Estudiantil Chicano de Aztlan, a Chicano student organization) in Albuquerque, New Mexico, along with 15 other students.

What happened at that conference was transformational. I saw a bunch of young people who looked like me going to college, celebrating their history, culture, and traditions, and advocating for equity and social justice. To say that it lit a fire in me is an understatement. All of us agreed on the bus ride home to start our own chapter of MEChA at our high school. We went on to create the largest student chapter in our state and host, plan, and run the first high school student conference. Our keynote speaker was Dolores Huerta, co-founder of the United Farm Workers Union with Cesar Chavez and one of the most influential social justice leaders of our time. She continues to be one of my greatest role models.

Leading Education with Love

The two individuals who not only gave us this opportunity but became the sponsors of our organization were Cristino and Mary Lou Griego. Cristino was our former principal, and Mary Lou was our librarian. They mentored us, inspired us, and taught us to stand up for what we believe in and do so with respect. And for many of us, they became a second set of parents. They had that unique ability to see our potential and set high expectations for us. They would teach us and remind us often about where we came from, the exceptional people whose blood we carry in our veins and the obstacles that our ancestors had overcome to get us to where we are today. Their wisdom and guidance led many of us into roles of advocacy and public service, but more than anything they helped us to see all that we were capable of and achieve it!

After graduating from college, I did finally move to the big city of Las Vegas, Nevada on luck and a prayer! I borrowed a thousand dollars from my cousin, rented a tiny U-Haul, and took off! I had sent resumes out and had interviews scheduled, but it was, in Vegas slang, a real crap shoot! I got there on Saturday, had interviews on Monday, and was working by Tuesday. Fast forward five years, I had completed my MBA, my career was taking off, and I had bought and sold my first home and bought my second home. I felt like all of the hard work was paying off but also like something was still missing. In the community where I grew up, giving back was just something we always did, whether it was helping the neighbor with their hay or animals or pulling over to help someone who was stuck on the side of the road. There was never a question if anyone was going to lend a hand; it's just what we did. I had to admit to myself that despite the individual achievements I was racking up, I was missing community. I felt a strong pull to get involved and give back. I was missing that sense of belonging and being a part of something bigger than me! I started out volunteering with organizations that fit my skills and passions, like Habitat for Humanity, since I grew up in the construction world.

I reconnected with a woman I had known in college, Sandra. We ended up being church buddies, and she became one of my biggest cheerleaders. Sandra introduced me to ALPFA, a Latino business professionals organization. I was once again with my community. The organization was full of young Latinx professionals who were doing big things! We grew the membership, and I went on to lead the chapter as President. In 2012, the chapter earned the national award for Small Chapter of the Year. My involvement in these community organizations gave me opportunities to get into the social circles that included other non-profit leaders and politicians.

At one of the events I was introduced to this rockstar young Latina who had recently been elected to the Nevada legislature, Lucy Flores. We became friends, and she began encouraging me to consider running for public office. My reaction was, "No way!" but she had planted a seed. At the time I was a couple of years into building my first company. I had started the company with my former boss, and we were doing great. Our company had grown from the two of us to over 20 in under two years. Unfortunately, my trusting heart and tendency to see the best in people meant I missed some red flags. My business partner pushed me out of the business after three years and we ended up in a very contentious legal battle. Again, my resilience (Chingona spirit) came through for me and I just started another busi-

Leading Education with Love

ness and kept right on going. My mentors, family and friends, the Griegos, Sandra, and Lucy were all there supporting me along the way.

While I backed away from the volunteer roles temporarily, I couldn't stay away for long. I started getting involved again, and every organization/non-profit I joined focused on education. Once again, I was "gently nudged" to run for office by several others, many of whom were either already serving or are doing so now. At the time, almost half of the students in our school district were Latinx and there wasn't anyone sitting at the table (School Board, State Board of Education, Regents, etc.) who looked like them. Someone needed to be their voice. That fire that MEChA had lit in me got sparked again!

I continued my advocacy work but still hesitated to run for office. The idea of politics sounded so exposing to me. But, they had "watered the seed" that Lucy had planted, and over time, I began warming up to the idea of running for office. One day three different people emailed me the same memo suggesting that I apply for the State Board of Education position. I remember clearly that I looked up and said "OK God I hear you!" I thought to myself, if this is what you want for me I will apply, and if it is meant for me, I will get the position. I said some prayers, applied for the position and sure enough, I got it.

That year was brutal! I was growing my new business, learning all about education policy and my new board role, *and* learning how to run a campaign while actually running a campaign. It was by far one of the hardest things I have ever done. I was determined to win, and I knocked on hundreds of doors, often alone. The scariest moment on the

Felicia Ortiz

campaign trail was having a guy threaten to shoot me for knocking on his door. My hands were shaking for a good ten minutes. There were days when I had to force myself out the door, but I kept going, and I won! I was the first Latina elected to the State Board of Education.

It didn't take long for me to realize just how badly my voice was needed. I spoke at school during my first year and the teacher sent me feedback from the students. One student said, "I had no idea a woman could be that successful, much less a Mexican woman!" I was floored! First of all, I didn't see myself as "that" successful, typical Empath behavior! I also know so many other super successful women from all ethnic backgrounds that I look up to and strive to emulate. I vowed to do all that I could to make sure all kids had positive role models to look up to and that I continued to be one for them. I was frequently lauded for asking hard questions and saying things people were thinking but not bringing up. That often confused me. Wasn't that why I was there? Most of the time I didn't think twice about asking because making sure kids got a quality education is the only priority for me. I truly felt like I was called to do this. It came naturally to me, and it fulfilled my deep desire to contribute to my community and society as a whole.

My fellow board members appreciated my perspective and actions, and they elected me President of the board right before the pandemic hit. We had just set aspirational goals for our state education system, and the world shut down. I remember sitting on my couch and crying. I was so worried about the students whose safe space is their school, the many students who depended on school for meals, and the families who were already barely hanging on financially.

Leading Education with Love

At first, the pandemic and how it was impacting education was overwhelming, but then the community came together in beautiful ways to help and support our students and educators. A few of us Latina advocates worked together to reach out to friends and family to get laptops donated to students in need. There was also an unprecedented public/private partnership between local gaming companies, the Public Education Foundation, the Department of Education, and Communities in Schools to ensure that our students had connectivity and devices. The best part was that everywhere you looked, social media, yard signs, and back windshields were messages of appreciation for our educators. As the months wore on the majority of teachers, students, and families were itching to get back into school buildings. The pandemic made all of us aware of how deeply we crave human connection.

Our schools are still grappling with the effects of our students missing out on valuable social and emotional development time with their teachers and peers. Everyone seems to agree that we need to do something different in education to ensure that students are getting all that they need to thrive in life. The system is pretty rigid and as we all know, change is *hard*, so most schools have gone right back to what we did before. What I've seen is that the focus went right back to academics, but we didn't address the trauma or give kids the opportunity to do what they missed most—have meaningful social interaction with their peers.

As I step into my final year as President of the NV State Board of Education, I am proud of how far we have come, but also frustrated by the lack of progress we have made. I know that my passion for education advocacy is not going away any time soon. We still have so many challenges to address:

- students are not coming to school like they did pre-pandemic;
- they are disengaged and dysregulated; teachers are leaving the profession in droves;
- and the skills and knowledge students need to be successful are changing rapidly with technology, artificial intelligence (AI), and an evolving job market.

My Dream of Heaven on Earth in Education

In my version of Heaven on Earth, the education system would look so much different than it does today! Let me tell you about my dream for education. In the "near future," all kids will be treated as if they are exceptional and given the opportunity, tools, and resources to succeed no matter where they were born, their socioeconomic status, abilities, or their race/ethnicity.

How We Teach

A lot of things will need to change, and I'll start with how we teach. In my Heaven on Earth, we meet all kids where they are, and each student has the opportunity to learn in the manner that suits them best and at the pace that suits them. Many of our schools are already implementing this model, known as Competency-Based Education and Differentiated Instruction, but the main barrier has been the ratio of teachers to students. One of the solutions is changing our teaching model. Rather than one teacher per classroom, each student has a team of adults that includes licensed teachers, social workers, support staff, and others who coach and guide them through their learning journey. This model is already being implemented successfully in Arizona thanks to ASU and Mesa School District.[1]

My hope is that this model reduces the individual burden on teachers and gives them opportunities to be innovative and creative and to bring back the joy of learning and teaching! I truly believe that Artificial Intelligence (I prefer to call it Assisted Intelligence) will be instrumental in making a lot of this possible, eliminating the overburdensome paperwork and planning so that teachers can do what they do best: teach! As students progress into junior high and high school, I envision them learning through experiences and projects versus sitting in a classroom reading aloud or getting a lecture. We will have opportunities for Career & Technical Education for every student. Students learning skills that they can immediately apply to their lives and future careers has proven to be one of the biggest success stories in Nevada, we just don't do enough of it...yet!

How We Evaluate

I would also address how we evaluate our students' success and hold the system and adults accountable. Gone are the high-stakes tests and letter grades for students and star ratings for schools. Students will "pass" their class when they master the content. If student A takes three months and student B takes three days, they both still learn all of the content so that they are successful in their next class or subject. This is especially important for reading and literacy as it is so foundational for all other subjects. Schools will be held accountable for ensuring students can demonstrate their learning in multiple ways. I see students learning through community-focused projects and demonstrating their knowledge in a portfolio of their work rather than just via tests. As students master content, they earn microcredentials that are transferable to industry credentials or college credits, something tangible that they can take with them and continue building on, regardless of whether they attend college, join the military, start a business, or go to a trade school.

How We Connect

Finally, I envision our community schools becoming just one of the many places students (of all ages) can learn. I want our students and their families to understand that learning happens all the time, so we as a community need to create as many opportunities as possible for learning to occur. Our country has a looming crisis with aging school buildings, while post-pandemic many commercial buildings sit empty. What if we used modern technology and AI to deal with logistics and transportation challenges and better utilize the space we already have? The majority of our schools sit empty for 16-18 hours a day. Why? One of the things that the pandemic taught us is that not all kids fare poorly in the online learning environment and that many kids like the flexibility that online learning provides. We must keep that option while still providing opportunities for social interaction and guided learning. All of this will require some major mindset shifts, but I believe it is possible.

I am working to make it a reality here in Nevada. I am part of a team in Nevada that is pushing for a new way of "doing" education. It is an approach that is focused on making sure our children are learning in an environment that empowers them to leverage their unique skills and abilities and helps them to build the communication and connection skills they need to thrive in their communities. Our goal is to foster their creativity and give them opportunities and experiences that allow them to demonstrate their academic knowledge in various ways. The best part is that most of this work is being driven by kids and the community, it is what they want!

My Personal Education Journey Continues

I signed up for Claudia's Empath Leader training as a way to keep learning and explore how my Empath Leadership could evolve. What it did was open up my eyes to my gifts and superpowers and provide an explanation for so many things that have happened in my life. I'll never forget the moment I knew I was an Empath. I was sitting in a restaurant when an older gentleman walked in with his family. When he went to sit in the booth, he missed the seat, fell to the floor, and started shaking. I felt his embarrassment and fear so deeply that I almost burst into tears. I could never explain that until now.

I also learned that the trauma I experienced in my youth was most likely the reason I am so aware of the energy around me at all times. What others have called my "inability to say no" or "people pleasing" is actually my intense desire to help and show love and support. My past lessons (what I used to refer to as failures) have taken on a new light. I realize that the Universe/God has put me on this path for a reason!

I spent three weeks this past summer on my ranch (my Heaven on Earth) in New Mexico reflecting on all that I

Felicia Ortiz

learned and where I want to go next. I have always been told, "You are so smart" or "You think differently and process so quickly," and I usually brushed it off. Now, I realize that my competence is one of the main reasons I have been so successful in school, in my career, and in business. My ability to create and maintain relationships is the other reason. People gravitate to me, and I love making connections. One of my favorite things to do is connect two people who can benefit from knowing one another! My ability to read the energy in the room and spot the person who is not being heard and call on them to give them a voice is another thing I've never put a lot of thought into, I realize now how rare and valuable that is. I am able to *feel* if someone is being authentic or not, which is super valuable in the political world.

The training also helped me to recognize when I need to set boundaries to protect my peace. While I love to be around others and thrive in public situations, it can also completely drain me. I have learned how to fill my cup through meditation and self-care. I am spending more time in New Mexico to ensure that I stay grounded and give myself rest. I've also started to get so much better at listening to my intuition and tuning into my psychic ability. It's pretty unreal how often it is spot on!

I am excited about what the future holds for me and my education advocacy journey. I look forward to writing a whole book about my next chapter of life and how my vision of Heaven on Earth for education became a reality. Stay tuned!

Meet Felicia Ortiz

Felicia Ortiz has served on the Nevada State Board of Education for the last 8 years, she has been President of the Board for the last 3 years. When she is not volunteering her time, she is a Project Management consultant. She played a critical role on the $9B CityCenter construction project in Las Vegas, Nevada that was the springboard for her starting a consulting firm.

In her chapter she explores how her childhood and upbringing have led her to these leadership roles and helped her to become an influential and trusted member of her community. She takes us on her journey into education advocacy and gives us her Heaven on Earth vision for the education system in our country.

Felicia is a Las Vegas native, twice over! She was born in Las Vegas, New Mexico (the Original) and currently resides in Las Vegas, Nevada! She finds peace and rejuvenation in nature, strolling with her beloved fur baby, Milagro. Her soul finds its sanctuary in her tiny home nestled on her ranch in New Mexico, a perfect retreat to recharge and stay grounded. Prepare to be inspired by Felicia's remarkable story, a journey of resilience, empathy, and unwavering dedication to making a difference!

Part Three
The Ultimate Empath Leadership Toolkit

Modalities for Enhancing Your Intuition and Connection to the Divine

I'm offering you options that serve as entryways to your intuition, and I forewarn you, the gist here is to point you towards *a* direction, not *the* direction. I have listed the modalities that I have used or tried, and are not in order of importance. Consider this the start of creating your very own ultimate Empath Leader toolkit.

With love,
Claudia

* * *

Traditional Meditation: Traditional meditation practices involve sitting in specific positions, focusing on the breath, and observing thoughts and sensations. These ancient techniques, such as Vipassana meditation and Zen Buddhism, have been proven effective for stress reduction, lowering blood pressure, and attaining transcendental states of awareness. They are also known in the West as Mindfulness practices. Some notable teachers that I learned from include Thich Nhat Hanh, Tara Brach, Jon Kabat-Zinn, and Rick Hanson, amongst many! Engaging in regular meditation and mindfulness exercises seek to quiet the mind, enhance self-awareness, and open channels to receive intuitive insights. By focusing attention on the present moment, we become more attuned to subtle signals – the whispers – from our intuition and the divine.

Active Meditations: Active meditations include instructions, visualizations, and physical engagement to facilitate self-inquiry and inner observation. My Dynamic Meditation Method, for example, offers a structured approach to self-inquiry while allowing folks to remain mobile, like in the case of walking meditations or while riding the bus. When I created this amalgam, it was birthed from the practices that had worked best for me and daily portability and practicality were crucial. I was aware that my clients with C-PTSD, ADHD, and General Anxiety would balk at the idea of sitting still with their unsupervised mind. I created a method that provided safety, self-reflection, and emotional decluttering, guided with questions. The Silva Method, developed by José Silva, focuses on enhancing intuition and psychic abilities through systematic training, as does Lester Levinson's Sedona Method.

Dreamwork: Dreamwork involves tapping into the subconscious mind during the theta and delta states of sleep to receive guidance and insights. By posing questions or intentions before sleep, you can access the wisdom of your dreams and decode symbolic messages. This modality can be a powerful tool for problem-solving and spiritual growth. Following the psychoanalytic masters Sigmund Freud and Carl Jung, I love using dream work in my psychotherapy sessions. Exploring and interpreting dreams can uncover hidden insights and messages from the subconscious or spiritual realms. I find it a way of studying our internal state of the union, wherein our higher self allows us to see what is and what's coming. We can receive our higher callings or purpose from our dreams; both the Dynamic Meditation Method and the Empath Leader Training came to me in dreams, in 2010 then 2020, respectively. John A. Sanford's and Morton T. Kelsey's work on dreams was quite influential in helping me to see God's messaging in dream states. Keeping a dream journal (I write down my dreams every morning), practicing lucid dreaming, and engaging in dream analysis techniques enhance intuition and deepen spiritual connection.

Intuitive Journaling: One of the anecdotal ways I recognize an Empath is by how they always have a journal. Clients who bring a notebook to a psychotherapy session or bring their own journal to my courses tend to be Empaths. Journaling is an Empath's best friend because we get to do all of our favorite things: profound thinking, intimate sharing, remembering, and integrating all that we have absorbed during the day or from an experience. Empaths naturally lean towards getting a PhD on themselves. Keeping a journal dedicated to intuitive insights, dreams, and synchronicities helps us recognize patterns and messages from the divine. Writing down thoughts and feelings without judgment can unlock deeper levels of intuition and spiritual connection for sure. Lee Harris, Empath, intuitive, and channeler, who does "The Energy Updates" on YouTube, suggests an exercise: Ask your Soul, "What do you want me to know today?" and wait for a response. When it comes, begin free writing.

Altered States Modalities: Dreamwork segways well into practices that induce altered states of consciousness, such as transcendental meditation, martial arts, Sufi dancing, and lucid dreaming. They provide avenues for transcending ordinary perception and accessing higher realms of awareness. These practices enable us to explore the depths of our psyche and connect with what feel like spiritual energies beyond the physical realm. I personally believe that tribal dancing, rave concerts, undisturbed driving for long periods of time, and singing in a group can induce altered states of consciousness.

Plant Medicine or Psychedelics: Plant medicine and psychedelics offer profound experiences that can catalyze spiritual awakening and personal transformation. While illegal in many jurisdictions, these substances have gained recognition for their therapeutic potential in treating trauma and facilitating profound insights. Several medicines – Ketamine, psilocybin, and MDMA – are used for trauma, depression, and anxiety, and with the exception of Ketamine which is legal, are in their last stages of FDA approval. Integrating these experiences with ongoing support and integration work is essential for maximizing their benefits. I do not recommend this modality without the presence of a knowledgeable guide or practitioner, a boundaried structure, an intention, a safe setting, and copious integration. Even though there are clinics that don't require this, I do.

Neurotraining: Neurotransmitter training, which involves placing electrodes on the head to modulate brain activity, has shown promise in enhancing meditation practices and inducing altered states of consciousness. However, this method can be costly and may not be accessible to all individuals. My favorite resource here is Daniel Siegel, a neuroscientist and clinical psychologist turned passionate meditator. Years ago he was charged with finding the parts of the brain that were impacted by meditation in the quest to find quicker ways of finding higher and peaceful states of consciousness. Originally a hard-core scientist and unbeliever, after executing his studies, Dr. Siegel is now a daily practitioner, a bestselling author, and the founder of the Mindsight Institute. His books focus on the neuroscientific relationship between the inner and outer worlds and between humans as it relates to mindfulness.

Breathwork: Breathwork techniques harness the power of conscious breathing to induce altered states and release emotional blockages. While highly effective for clearing the mind and body, breathwork can lead to intense emotional releases and requires careful facilitation. Despite its nonmethodical nature, breathwork remains a potent tool for inner transformation. If you haven't been exposed to breathwork, it is not your run-of-the-mill box breathing. Deep breath work can feel like a psychedelic experience, and buried trauma can resurface for release. I recommend the same standards for breathwork that I do for psychedelics.

Tarot and Oracle Cards: Tarot and oracle cards are known as tools for tapping into intuition and receiving guidance from the divine. Even if you don't believe in Tarot, or don't understand the cards, take them as symbolic messages, like a fable, myth, or multiple sightings of a sequence of numbers. Through contemplation of card imagery and symbolism, you can access deeper insights into your life path and spiritual journey. In psychodynamic psychotherapy, we try to understand the images or "signs" a person encounters through their personal associations. Even though each card has a symbolic meaning, you can combine that meaning with your individual association – what does this mean to you?

Energy Work: Practices such as Reiki, Qigong, and Pranic Healing focus on balancing and manipulating subtle energies within the body. By clearing blockages, aligning energetic pathways, and engaging the body, receptivity to intuitive messages and spiritual guidance are embedded. Around for centuries in the East, your willingness to open up to the gifts of these practices is already an intuitive hit.

Nature Connection: Non-negotiable, no-brainer! Spending time in nature can foster a deep sense of connection to the divine and facilitate intuitive insights. Whether through hiking, gardening, or simply sitting in quiet contemplation, immersing oneself in natural surroundings can evoke a sense of awe and interconnectedness. We are nature, we coexist with nature, and nature is our parent. Our central nervous systems automatically rest and align when we gaze at the sky, see water, notice the colors of trees, or feel the silence of falling snow. Even for us, born and raised as city-dwellers, watering our plants, walking our dogs, sitting in a hot bath, are all forms of reconnecting to natural elements of this planetary existence. Nature is an intuitive hack!

Ritual and Ceremony: In my monthly psycho-spiritual roundtable, Wealth from Within, and in the Empath Leader training, I require that folks have what I call "RICHuals". I propose slowing down and transforming routine daily tasks into RICHuals; it changes our whole approach to the ordinary. Rituals and ceremonies performed with reverence can create sacred space and invite divine presence through their intention alone. Whether through personal rituals or participation in community ceremonies, we can cultivate a deeper connection to the divine and amplify their intuitive abilities. One of the RICH parts of RICHual is sharing them in the community. Ritual and ceremony is part of what makes us human and provide deep belonging.

Sound Healing: There is so much more scientific data on the effect of sound on our emotional well-being. Sound healing modalities such as chanting, singing bowls, and drumming harmonize body, mind, and spirit and facilitate deep states of relaxation and receptivity. The vibrational frequencies produced by sound can help us attune to higher realms of consciousness and intuitive guidance. We know that music, for example, can shift our moods, put us into trance states, time travel us to a heartbreak or a party in 1999, and help us write a book (wink-wink). One of my favorite sources is Dr. Masaru Emoto's New York Times bestselling book, the *Hidden Messages in Water*, wherein he studied the effects of sound on water in his claim that human consciousness can affect the molecular structure of water.

Visualization and Creative Expression: Engaging in visualization exercises and creative expression, such as art, music, or dance, are a powerful stimulating source for the imagination and the activation of intuitive insights. Millennia of tapping into the subconscious mind and the realm of symbolism, tracing back to early hominid caves, furnished us with access to deeper layers of intuition and spiritual wisdom. The idea of describing what visualization, art, dance, and creative expression has done for humanity and explaining that they all involve connection to higher realms, just exhausts me in its vastness. The plethora of examples seem endless. Instead, I recommend you visit the Museum of Modern Art in NYC and the Louvre in Paris, gaze at the Sistine Chapel in the Vatican, watch the Alvin Ailey dance troupe, read Mary Oliver, Hafiz, and E.E. Cummings, and top it off with a Shakespearean verse with Mozart's Concerto Piano 21 in the background. It is Soul eroticism at its best – otherworldliness is inescapable!

Incorporating these modalities to enhance your spiritual practice can support the cultivation of intuition and foster a deeper connection to the divine, guiding you on your journey of self-discovery and spiritual growth. Experiment with different techniques to find what resonates most deeply with your own unique path and inner wisdom. Each of these modalities offers unique pathways for raising intuition and deepening connection to the divine. Exploring a combination of practices and seeking guidance from experienced practitioners and fellow walkers can help you discover the modalities that resonate most deeply with you.

Claudisms

A collection of terms coined by Claudia Cauterucci

trauma rising

A way of existing wherein we make the conscious and deliberate choice to use our wounded past — our trauma — and alchemize it into a powerful and dynamic NOW life. We believe that our wounds can be our gifts.

thank you triggers

We say "thank you" triggers because they highlight the unconscious places where we still need to heal. Our triggers allow us to clean up our old, wounded programming.

party of one

Is the profile of the child that survived taking care of themselves, bypassed their own needs, & spent many nights ruminating on how to solve things they didn't understand. They turn into high achievers because they were on overdrive as parental problem-solvers. As adults, they feel internally alone often.

***

party of two-niverse

Is when the party of one adult heals and loves their inner child. They finally believe that they are not alone and have faith that there is a higher power, a loving universe, a community, or another person who is in their corner and from whom they will receive support and encouragement.

s.y.a.d.

When you get triggered, are anxious, feel overwhelmed, are whiplashed by external events, SYAD -- sit your ass down! Harness your power by plopping down, engaging your breathing, & meditating, rather than moving into action. SYAD is your highest form of action.

one over one

The fraction $+1/+1$ = POSITIVE ONE The fraction $+1/-1$ = NEGATIVE ONE Even if you're succeeding & are a high achiever, what's your bottom fraction? Are you achieving due to fear, guilt, or shame? WHAT'S YOUR FUEL SOURCE? Is it positive or negative? What's your bottom fraction?

yesssssshale

In the Dynamic Meditation Method, we acknowledge and release our feelings by saying yes to them. We inhale then we yessssssshale them out.

* * *

re-pair

Red wine is paired with meat. White wine is paired with fish. Beer is paired with wings.

Memories are paired with emotions.

Through healing, we RE-PAIR our memories with new emotions.

the volumes

VOLUME 1 The story you were born into. You are unconscious and swallowing what you're taught undigested.

VOLUME 2 You're awakening moments. These can be beautiful and they can be hard. You are no longer unconscious.

VOLUME 3 Your chosen story. You consciously decide & design your life.

favorite version

I naturally love the concept of growing into the highest version of ourselves.

But living into the favorite version of ourselves feels most enlivening, coherent, intimate, and..."cute."

"Cuteness" is tenderness, a key component of human intimacy.

possibility

Possibility is human magic. Possibility is what makes our life exciting, erotic, and alive. Possibility designs a future.

Trauma steals possibility. When we transmute trauma we bring back possibility.

POSSIBILITY IS THE GENIE IN THE BOTTLE.

your story is not my story

When you get triggered, are anxious, feel overwhelmed, are whiplashed by external events, SYAD -- sit your ass down! Harness your power by plopping down, engaging your breathing, & meditating, rather than moving into action. SYAD is your highest form of action.

otté

The healing sequence we use in the Dynamic Meditation Method.

- Observe: We acknowledge the triggers, the wounds, & the patterns
- Transmute: We heal them internally first with our tools
- Transform: We change who we are in the external world
- Evolve: We grow & up level

colorful person

A term I have given myself in a world full of dynamic, beautiful color. As a global Latina, I feel that the term "person of color" sets me apart, while Colorful person includes me with all my essence, rhythm, movement, expressiveness, and passion. * And you too *

* * *

the 4 p's

pause FOR power FOR possibility FOR prowess

triple d's

discover THEN discern THEN decide

shameless

Shameless means de-shaming!

We are de-shaming need, intimacy, sexuality, and sensuality.

Need keeps our humanity together.

Intimacy is our mammalian love language.

Sexuality ignites expansion.

Sensuality embodies living.

Shameless, a life free from shame.

Acknowledgments

Thank you to my entire team at Soul Excellence Publishing for helping to make this shared dream a reality.

The team who came together to create this book represents Empaths beginning to find their long-lost tribe and collaborating using their psychic and creative gifts.

* * *

First and foremost, thank you to **Kecia Bal**, our editor, who the Universe brought to us in our time of need, close to the end of the manuscript when Claudia and I could no longer imagine how this book would read to a new member of the Empath tribe. Kecia came into the project with an Empath's compassion, competence, and conviction, and using her gifts brought clarity and conciseness to the book. There is no one else Claudia and I could imagine having worked with to bring *The Empath Leader* to life. I met Kecia over two years ago, and she instantly earned my trust and admiration for saying yes to partnering in unique ways to support my authors. We have partnered on several of Soul Excellence's books, but this feels like our greatest masterpiece to date, and we are so grateful for you. Thank you, Kecia.

You can work with Kecia by connecting with her on LinkedIn: https://www.linkedin.com/in/keciabal/

* * *

Thank you to **Kelly Fischer**, Founder of Depth Theory, a boutique conscious marketing firm, for bringing our vision of the fiery and kind heart to life through our social media graphics and a book launch plan that provided so much secure attachment for this group of authors to feel safe and supported as we become more visible and vocal. I first met Kelly at an in-person local event for creative entrepreneurs, and I was struck by her optimism and, yes, depth. We've since collaborated on three, now four, Soul Excellence Publishing bestselling book launches together, where she has always translated the energy of the book and spirit of the authors into alluring visuals (a talent that I deeply admire) and clear, mission-aligned copy. Thank you, Kelly.

You can work with Kelly by visiting Depth Theory: https://www.depththeory.com/

* * *

Thank you to **Kristina Brummer**, Founder of The Spectacular Middle, for supporting the behind-the-scenes work that turns a manuscript into an actual book! I met Kristina four years ago in an online entrepreneur program as we both made the conscious decision to step away from corporate lives and dive head-first into our own creative expressions. Book after book, Kristina has shown up to make sure Soul Excellence's publications live up to the highest standards and our publishing and marketing processes go smoothly. Thank you, Kristina.

You can work with Kristina by visiting The Spectacular Middle: https://www.thespectacularmiddle.com/

* * *

Thank you to **Hamdan Nasrullah,** our book cover designer. Like everyone I am thanking, Hamdan has helped bring multiple Soul Excellence Publishing books to life, each with its own personality, but each connected to our brand ethos of equal parts strength and softness. You outdid yourself on this one, making the fire-heart emoji come to life and helping us activate our root chakras through the vibrant red and gold color scheme.

You can work with Hamdan by visiting his portfolio on 99Designs: https://99designs.com/profiles/hamdanas

* * *

Thank you for a job well done and full of heart!

Kayleigh O'Keefe

Founder and CEO, Soul Excellence Publishing

Bibliography
& Endnotes

Alcoholics Anonymous. *Alcoholics Anonymous: The Story of How Many Thousands of Men and Women Have Recovered from Alcoholism*. 4th ed. New York: Alcoholics Anonymous World Services, Inc., 2001.

Being, Grace. "Self Healing from Narcissistic Abuse: The Power of Mindset." Grace Being, September 25, 2023. https://grace-being.com/love-relationships/self-healing-from-narcissistic-abuse/.

Brach, Tara. *Radical Acceptance: Embracing Your Life With the Heart of a Buddha*. Reprint ed. Bantam, November 23, 2004.

Brown, Brené. *Daring Greatly: How the Courage to Be Vulnerable Transforms the Way We Live, Love, Parent, and Lead*. Gotham Books, 2012.

De Rosa, Wendy. *Becoming an Empowered Empath: How to Clear Energy, Set Boundaries & Embody Your Intuition*. Foreword by Gabrielle Bernstein. Paperback. March 30, 2021.

Durvasula, Ramani. *Should I Stay or Should I Go?: Surviving a Relationship with a Narcissist*. Kindle ed. Post Hill Press, November 24, 2015. ASIN: B016989HIW.

Flaker, Amanda. Amanda Flaker. YouTube. Accessed 2023. https://www.youtube.com/c/amandaflaker.

Foundation for Inner Peace. *A Course in Miracles*. 3rd ed. Mill Valley: Foundation for Inner Peace, June 14, 2022.

Hanh, Thich Nhat. *The Art of Living: Peace and Freedom in the Here and Now*. Reprint ed. HarperOne, April 4, 2023.

Bibliography

Hanson, Rick, with Richard Mendius. *Buddha's Brain: The Practical Neuroscience of Happiness, Love, and Wisdom*. Illustrated ed. First Edition. New Harbinger Publications, November 1, 2009.

Harris, Lee. *Energy Speaks: Messages from Spirit on Living, Loving, and Awakening*. Foreword by Regina Meredith. New World Library, March 26, 2019.

Harris, Lee, and Dianna Edwards. *Conversations with the Z's, Book One: The Energetics of the New Human Soul*. Conversations with the Z's, 1. New World Library, September 13, 2022.

Kabat-Zinn, Jon. *Wherever You Go, There You Are: Mindfulness Meditation in Everyday Life*. 10th ed. Hachette Books, January 5, 2005.

Kelsey, Morton T. *God, Dreams, and Revelation: A Christian Interpretation of Dreams*. Revised and Expanded Edition. Fortress Press, January 1, 1991.

Levenson, Lester, and Hale Dwoskin. *Happiness Is Free: And It's Easier Than You Think, Books 1 through 5, The Greatest Secret Edition*. Foreword by Rhonda Byrne. Sedona Press, October 13, 2020.

Levenson, Lester. *No Attachments, No Aversions: The Autobiography of a Master*. Sherman Oaks: Lawrence Crane Enterprises, Inc., January 1, 2023.

Orloff, Judith, M.D. *The Empath's Survival Guide: Life Strategies for Sensitive People*. Hardcover. January 1, 2017.

Roberts, Jane. *The Seth Material*. Englewood Cliffs, NJ: Prentice-Hall, 1970.

Romano, Lisa A. *The Road Back to Me: Healing and Recovering from Codependency, Addiction, Enabling, and Low Self Esteem*. Kindle ed. Published by Lisa A. Romano, April 12, 2012.

Bibliography

Silva, José. *The Silva Mind Control Method.* Kindle ed. Gallery Books, November 8, 2022.

Sinek, Simon. *Leaders Eat Last: Why Some Teams Pull Together and Others Don't.* Portfolio, 2016.

Sol, Mateo, and Aletheia Luna. *Awakened Empath: The Ultimate Guide to Emotional, Psychological and Spiritual Healing.* CreateSpace Independent Publishing Platform, October 2017.

Walsch, Neale Donald. *Conversations with God: An Uncommon Dialogue, Book 1.* New York: G.P. Putnam's Sons, 1996.

Endnotes

Chapter 2 - Meet The Empath
Rumi. *Selected Poems.* Translated by Coleman Barks with John Moynce, A. J. Arberry, Reynold Nicholson. Penguin Books, 2004.

Chapter 5 - Self-Care: Your Survival Kit
Walcott, Derek. "Love After Love." In *Collected Poems 1948-1984*, 354-355. New York: Farrar, Straus and Giroux, 1986.

Chapter 6 - What Kind of Psychic Are You?

1. "Psychic." In *Cambridge Dictionary*. Accessed December 8, 2023. https://dictionary.cambridge.org/us/dictionary/english/psychic.
2. Aristotle. *The Philosophy of Aristotle.* Translated by Renford Bambrough, with an introduction and notes by A. E. Wardman. Signet Classics.
3. Shayne, Tasha. "Is Quantum Entanglement the Key to Spiritual Ascension?" Gaia, February 18, 2021. https://www.gaia.com/article/is-quantum-entanglement-the-key-to-spiritual-ascension.

Bibliography

Chapter 7 - Leadership and The Rise of The Meek

1. D'Auria, Gemma, and Aaron De Smet. "Leadership in a Crisis: Responding to the Coronavirus Outbreak and Future Challenges." McKinsey & Company, March 16, 2020. https://www.mckinsey.com/capabilities/people-and-organizational-performance/our-insights/leadership-in-a-crisis-responding-to-the-coronavirus-outbreak-and-future-challenges.
2. Miller, Kelsey. "The Triple Bottom Line: What It Is & Why It's Important." Harvard Business School Online, December 8, 2020. https://online.hbs.edu/blog/post/what-is-the-triple-bottom-line.
3. Preble, Will. "Empathic Leadership: Why Empaths Need to Lead." LinkedIn, October 13, 2021. https://www.linkedin.com/pulse/empathic-leadership-why-empaths-need-lead-will-preble/

Chapter 15 - Human Piñata

Chapman, Canaan. "The Upside-Down Kingdom." He Reads Truth, April 25, 2023. https://hereadstruth.com/2023/04/25/the-upside-down-kingdom/.

Chapter 16 - Leading Education With Love

Flannery, Shelley. "What Happens When a Class Has 5 Teachers?" ASU News, January 2, 2024. https://news.asu.edu/20240102-arizona-impact-what-happens-when-class-has-5-teachers.

Also By Soul Excellence Publishing

Since 2020, Soul Excellence Publishing has amplified the wisdom of conscious, courageous leaders from around the globe charting the path to a New Earth.

Featured titles:

- *The Diversity in Humanity: A New Vision for Harmony in the Workplace*
- *The Great LeadHERship Awakening*
- *The Queen Bee: Embody Your Truth and Live Fully Expressed*
- *The X-Factor: The Spiritual Secrets Behind Successful Executives & Entrepreneurs*
- *Black Utah: Stories from a Thriving Community*
- *Significant Women: Leaders Reveal What Matters Most*
- *Leading Through the Pandemic: Unconventional Wisdom from Heartfelt Leaders*

Please visit our website to see all of our trailblazing publications and authors.

https://soulexcellence.com/

Made in the USA
Middletown, DE
14 April 2024